Praise for *Shift*

"Tomorrow arrives, each day, whether or not we're ready for it. This profound book of wisdom will help identify the seven mindset shifts that open the door for new possibilities as we lead into our future."
SETH GODIN, author of *The Song of Significance*

"A book that treats midlife not as a decline, but as the bold adventure it should be. Peter Reek's seven shifts will change how you see aging and yourself."
MICHAEL BUNGAY STANIER, bestselling author of
The Coaching Habit and *How to Work with (Almost) Anyone*

"*Shift* is a terrific book! I didn't read it so much as sink into it. I feel changed by the experience. Midlife now comes with a manual. *Shift* is thoughtful, hopeful, and refreshingly practical about what it takes to grow through change."
PETER BREGMAN, bestselling author of *18 Minutes* and
Leading with Emotional Courage

"Midlife isn't a crisis—it's a catalyst. In *Shift*, Peter Reek invites readers to reimagine this pivotal life stage as a time of reinvention, purpose, and profound personal growth. I believe it shines a vital light on how the physical, emotional, and hormonal changes of this life phase—especially for women—reshape our relationships, identities, and ambitions. It creates a path to living inspired in the second half of life."
DR. JESSICA SHEPHERD, board-certified gynecologist and menopause expert, author of *Generation M*

"What is time, anyway? Peter Reek understands this: that time is just time, and how old you are, what stage you're at in the game, or how many years you have left are just a number in your head—real, but not that big of a deal, because at any point, you can begin again. You can cook it up all over again, you can step into the unknown with joy and, no matter how much you're trembling, with the assurance that you're going to be fine."

ROB BELL, *New York Times*-bestselling author of fourteen books including *Love Wins*

"This book felt like a conversation I didn't know I needed. *Shift* reminds us that change doesn't start with a plan—it starts with a mindset. Peter Reek offers a deeply human invitation to rethink what's possible when we loosen old definitions and imagine life on new terms. A wise, soulful, and beautifully written guide for anyone ready to reframe their story and answer, 'Who am I now?'"

CATHERINE DUCHARME, founder and principal of Fluency Leadership

SHIFT

7 Mindsets for an *Inspired Midlife*

SHIFT

PETER REEK

PAGE TWO

Copyright © 2025 by Peter Reek

All rights reserved. No part of this book may be reproduced, stored in a retrieval system or transmitted, in any form or by any means, without the prior written consent of the publisher, except in the case of brief quotations, embodied in reviews and articles.

InHabit.LifeTM is a trademark owned by Peter Reek

Some names and identifying details have been changed to protect the privacy of individuals.

This book is not intended as a substitute for the medical advice of physicians. The reader should regularly consult a physician in matters relating to their health and particularly with respect to any symptoms that may require diagnosis or medical attention.

Cataloguing in publication information is available from Library and Archives Canada.
ISBN 978-1-77458-650-1 (paperback)
ISBN 978-1-77458-731-7 (ebook)

Page Two
pagetwo.com

Page Two™ is a trademark owned by Page Two Strategies Inc., and is used under license by authorized licensees

Cover and interior design by Cameron McKague

shiftintomidlife.com

Dedicated to my friend, Malcolm Cameron

SOME PEOPLE come into your life and rearrange the furniture—not in a loud, disruptive way, but with quiet wisdom, making space for something better. Malcolm Cameron was that kind of person. He didn't just show up; he shifted perspectives, made room for hope, and left every place—and every person—better than he found them.

We met at university, where he was the campus chaplain. But Malcolm was never just a title. He had a rare ability to see past limitations and uncover potential. When he opened his counseling practice, he created a place where thousands found healing, simply because he believed in them.

His journey with early onset Alzheimer's was devastating. Watching someone you love fade like that is a loss beyond words. His wife, Sandy, and his children, MacKenzie and Brayden, carried him through it with extraordinary love and grace. His absence is felt in ways big and small, in stories unfinished and spaces left empty.

Midlife has a way of forcing us to rearrange the furniture. Sometimes by choice, sometimes by necessity. We lose people. Plans change. The world shifts under our feet. The real question isn't whether change will happen; it's whether we'll have the courage to adapt, to make space for what's next, and to keep going.

As I launch the counseling center at InHabit.Life, I had imagined Malcolm by my side. That won't happen in the way I expected. But his presence is still here—in the foundation of this work and in the belief that people can find their way forward.

This book is for you, my friend. Your light lives on.

The Shift

The years come on tiptoes,
not brash or bold, but certain,
easing into the small spaces
we didn't know we'd made.
They settle in, reshuffling
the familiar mess,
making a path where we couldn't see one.
We notice what's faded—
our stretch, our speed,
the easy laughter echoing long—
but look closer. Something else is growing
where that used to be:
quiet afternoons held like breath,
a routine that's fit like an old friend,
a steady pulse of what truly matters.
Aging isn't a thief;
it's a careful hand, pruning what's wild,
coaxing what's enduring.

We start to savor what's small—
a book, a walk, the company of those
who've stuck around.
And yes, there's still the mess—
but it's a holy mess, sacred in its sprawl,
proof of a life not pruned too far,
a life lived and left in corners,
unruly, unapologetic.
The future doesn't pound at the door;
it nudges quietly, not with loud assertions
but soft assurances of what's to come.
And so we shift,
not into fireworks or sparks,
but into joy, worn smooth and wide,
the joy of something that's lasted—
of something that still fits just right.

CONTENTS

Foreword by Chip Conley *1*
Preface: How *Shift* Was Born *3*
Introduction: Setting the Stage *7*

PART ONE — PREPARING TO SHIFT

1. Life in Two Halves:
   The Art of Becoming *29*
2. Mindset and Midlife:
   The Lens That Changes Everything *41*
3. The Second-Half Advantage:
   The View from "Over the Hill" *53*
4. Looking Inward to Look Outward *65*
5. Navigating Midlife's Derailers:
   Owning the Plot Twists *73*

PART TWO — THE THREE CORE COMMITMENTS

6. Commitment One:
   Lead Your Whole Self Well *85*
7. Commitment Two:
   Tell Yourself the Truth *99*
8. Commitment Three:
   Practice Radical Acceptance *115*

PART THREE — THE SEVEN MINDSET SHIFTS

9 Shift into Curiosity:
Release the Shackles of Certainty *131*

10 Shift into Connection:
You Aren't Meant to Do This Alone *145*

11 Shift into Response-Ability:
The Pause That Changes Things *161*

12 Shift into Alignment:
Sync with What Matters *185*

13 Shift into Befriending Your Body:
The Companion That's Brought
You Here *207*

14 Shift into Stillness:
The World Won't Stop, but You Can *223*

15 Shift into Brave:
Cultivate the Courage to Shift *235*

Conclusion:
This Is Just the Beginning *255*

Acknowledgments *259*

Notes *261*

FOREWORD

WE ARE GROWING OLD in a fascinating era in which we're living longer in a world that is changing faster than ever before. How do we stay relevant in a society that is vastly different from the one our parents encountered? I learned quite a bit about this when I became the in-house mentor to the young Airbnb founders early in their career and became known as the "modern elder" of the company (according to them, "someone as curious as they are wise"). This led me to create the world's first midlife wisdom school, the Modern Elder Academy (MEA).

So, you can imagine my joy when I was introduced to Peter Reek's work and writing. He's helped us to see that our era offers us a rich and meaningful exploration of what it means to step into the second half of life with courage and intention. I love this book as it's grounded in something solid—science, research, and practical wisdom—woven together with stories that will resonate deeply. I found it a compelling read and will be adding it to the libraries of each of our MEA campuses.

Some of my favorite concepts from the book include the three core commitments. When Peter says to "lead your whole self well," he stresses that because every part of you—spiritual, mental, emotional, social, and physical—works together in sync; you can't ignore those parts. I also appreciated his explanation of radical acceptance. It involves embracing your story not as a resignation, but as a powerful way to move forward with freedom and hope. As I read this sage advice, I felt like I had a world-class expert by my side.

Because this book isn't a bunch of platitudes, I appreciated the specificity of the seven mindset shifts we need in midlife and beyond. This is such a foundational part of living a good, healthy life, because as we age, many of us get calcified in our fixed mindsets.

This book is written from a perspective that feels both personal and authoritative. Peter is like your best friend who is also an expert in living a vital second half of life. Upon reading this, you'll feel such warmth, insight, and humor from Peter while he makes big concepts feel actionable. The second half of our life, as defined by all kinds of studies, isn't all about decline. It's also a time for developing a renewed sense of purpose based upon our hard-won wisdom. This book is an invitation—not a map with rigid directions, but a compass pointing toward what's possible. By purchasing this book, you've taken the first step toward consciously curating a second adulthood that is full of emotional well-being, relational connection, and spiritual curiosity.

I hope you enjoy *Shift* as much as I did.

CHIP CONLEY
Founder and Executive Chair,
Modern Elder Academy

PREFACE
HOW *SHIFT* WAS BORN

WHEN I WAS EIGHTEEN, I packed up my life in Toronto and headed west to Vancouver for university. I didn't overthink it—it was one of those moments when you just take a step and see where it leads. I studied the mechanics of how the world works—economics, marketing, law—but it was my English classes, with their focus on stories and the human condition, that lit me up. I didn't know it then, but I was already being drawn to the thread that would run through everything that came next: an enduring fascination with people and what makes us who we are.

After university, I started in human resources, pulled toward the people side of business. Later, I shifted into marketing and discovered another lens for understanding human behavior. My career brought me incredible opportunities—helping launch businesses in the UK and Australia, then founding a consultancy focused on branding and connection. Eventually, I ran a marketing-focused search firm and conducted over six thousand interviews. I always began by asking, "So, you were born. Then what?" Not to map a career trajectory—but to understand the moments that shape a life.

Those conversations stayed with me. Patterns emerged. And one truth kept surfacing: Mindset matters. The most fulfilled people weren't coasting through life or waiting for the perfect timing. They were choosing growth. Reinventing. Paying attention. That realization lodged itself deep.

Seventeen years into my business, I felt the pull to go deeper. I sold the company and returned to school, earning a master's degree in applied positive psychology and coaching. My research centered on midlife transition and uncovered what I had already started to suspect: Mindset is not just important—it's predictive. It shapes how we interpret change, how we move through uncertainty, and how we imagine what's possible next.

That's how *Shift* came together. Not with a detailed plan, but as something that emerged over time—from questions I kept hearing, stories I couldn't forget, and lessons I was learning myself. I came to see that the real turning points in life are often quiet. They show up as questions that won't leave us alone or patterns we finally get honest enough to name.

What struck me—both in the research and in my own experience—is how much of our future is shaped by mindset. How we explain change to ourselves. How we respond when things don't go as planned. Some people get stuck; others grow. And more often than not, the difference isn't what happens to us. It's how we think about it, how we pay attention, and what we're willing to learn along the way.

One of the biggest surprises in writing this book is that I rediscovered poetry. Writing poetry showed me something new: Not everything important needs to be explained right away. Some things are meant to be felt first. They need a little time to settle in before we try to make sense of them. In a world wired for instant answers, poetry reminded me that some truths work on a different clock.

That's the spirit behind *Shift*. I wrote it because I've seen how mindset shapes a life—slowly, steadily; one thought and one choice at a time. When we stop rushing, allow ourselves to feel, start listening, and open our minds, things can begin to shift.

INTRODUCTION
SETTING THE STAGE

Salt and Light

It happens like this:
One day you're reaching for the salt,
thinking about how it's almost time
to clean the gutters,
and then, just like that,
you notice the way the light
falls across the kitchen table,
turning it into something
worth writing about.

You find yourself pausing—
mid-reach, mid-thought, mid-life—
wondering how many other moments
you've missed
while thinking of things that,
let's be honest,
could wait.

Your focus shifts,
not because you want to—
who has time to ponder
the familiar shape of your favorite mug,
or the scent of rain on pavement—
but because, suddenly,
you can't not.

And, you begin to see,
really see,
the small things that were always there,
like the way your old cedar
leans a little more each year
or how the dog sighs,
as if he too knows
the quiet weight of time.

You might even chuckle
at the absurdity of it all—
this sudden shift in focus,
as if the universe has conspired
to slow you down,
to nudge you toward
the poetry in the everyday.

Then again,
maybe that's the point,
that all these small things—
the overlooked, the unseen—
were the big things all along,
waiting for you to catch up,
to shift,
and see.

The Invitation

The second half of your life: Here it is, unfolding before you, rich with promise, mystery, and, yes, its own set of challenges.

In the first part of life, we strive and stretch and reach. We chase success, build things, prove ourselves, and slowly piece together who we are. But the second half whispers a different kind of invitation. It's less about climbing and more about returning. Returning to what matters, to who we've always been. It's the season where we start to notice what age gives us rather than what it takes away. Strength shows up in vulnerability. Freedom takes root in discipline. And somehow, there's peace to be found in the not knowing.

Yes, the second half will bring challenges, but it also holds a promise of simplicity. It's in savoring the warmth of the sun on your face, the joy of a deep conversation, the thrill of discovering something new about yourself or rekindling an old passion. Midlife is about uncovering the extraordinary in ordinary moments and recognizing just how much these moments matter.

Here's a truth: The richness of midlife doesn't just happen. It's something you create with your own hands, heart, and mind. This chapter isn't written by fate; it's crafted by the choices you make and the mindset you bring along the way. In midlife the plot twists, the main character deepens, and the story starts to get really interesting. You're holding the pen here, and you're the star of this story. So, what kind of life will you create for yourself? What scenes, what dreams, will you bring to life on these pages?

How you approach aging shapes how you navigate the changes ahead. Despite the years that have added layers of experience, your mind remains incredibly powerful. Sure, there are days it might feel like it needs a jumpstart, but don't underestimate its strength. Too often, we're taught to see life in black-and-white, right-or-wrong terms. This thinking may work for simple choices, but it falls short when it comes to life's big questions. Midlife invites you to lean into nuance and find growth in the gray areas, where the real beauty of life unfolds.

This book calls you to focus on what truly matters—to live each day with intention, grace, and the kind of authenticity that lights up your soul. And if you've made it this far, you've gained some wisdom along the way. You know that measuring twice saves headaches and that wearing white to a barbecue is a calculated risk. You learn over time that, some days, you grip the wheel with both hands and steer into the storm. Some days, you roll down the windows, let the wind tangle your hair, and trust the ride.

Consider this your invitation to approach life with curiosity, adventure, and a renewed sense of wonder. Let the second half of your life unfold like a classic film that only gets richer with each viewing. Because, as with any great story, there's room for laughter, a few tears, and everything in between.

Shaping Our Own Path

So, what's next? How do we navigate midlife when the path ahead is anything but clear? Here's what we know: Clarity and action are our strengths, and we define success on our own terms.

Defining success differently: Success has always been a bit slippery. We chase it, we name it, we compare ours to someone else's, and then we wonder why it still doesn't quite land. At some point, usually after enough striving and late-night overthinking, we begin to ask different questions. Not just, "Am I successful?" but something deeper. Writer Rich Cohen put it this way: "The work was not wasted. It was the hassle and hustle [of life] that made you arrive at the only question worth trying to answer: What do I really want?" That line gets me every time. Because somewhere in the middle of the mess and momentum, we start to let go of an old dream. Not because we failed, but because we've grown. And from there, something new can begin.

Embracing our resilience: Resilience isn't something we discovered later in life. It has been baked into us from the start. We were the latchkey kids, learning to navigate the world on our own before we even knew what that meant. We've lived through recessions, shifting norms, broken systems, and global upheaval, and we're still here. Still showing up. Elwood Watson said it well: "Generation Xers have survived and, in some cases, thrived in the face of unrelenting adversity. This tenacity has equipped many of us with the adaptability needed to handle life's uncertainties." That sounds about right. We've been adapting since the beginning. It's what we do.

Staying solution-focused: We're resilient, but we're also practical. When challenges arise, we don't get bogged down in blame; we roll up our sleeves and get to work. Pragmatic, resourceful, and relentless, we keep pushing forward—traits that will serve us well as we navigate midlife.

Moving forward with purpose: The road ahead may be bumpy, but we're equipped with the experience and wisdom that come from facing challenges head-on. Now is the time to lean into that wisdom, lead with purpose, and make the second half of our lives as meaningful and impactful as the first—maybe even more so.

So, how do we approach midlife? With clarity and conviction. We have the chance to redefine this stage of life—not just for ourselves but for those who follow. Social scientist Arthur Brooks captures this perfectly when he encourages us to focus on what aging gives rather than what it takes away. Midlife isn't a decline. It's a time to grow, refine strengths, and create a greater impact. Our best days are in front of us.

But to truly embrace midlife, we must look to inhabit it. Not just pass through it, not just survive it—but to fully *live* in it. To show up with presence, curiosity, and care. To bring our whole selves—our questions, our dreams, our scars, and our hope—into our unfolding story.

You might think there's some secret formula for thriving in this stage of life. There isn't. But here's what we know: It's all about your mindset. How you approach aging can make all the difference. What if you stopped seeing it as a loss and started seeing it as a gain—of wisdom, perspective, even freedom? That's what this journey is: embracing the opportunities and gifts that come with this season of life. First, I'll encourage you to zero in on what really matters. Then we'll set three core commitments and make seven mindset shifts. Here's a preview.

Three Core Commitments

The journey to a richer, more fulfilling second half starts with three key commitments. They're the foundation for the change you're hoping to create. Break them, and progress gets harder. Honor them, and you'll build momentum. Let's commit to showing up for ourselves—it's the first step toward real transformation.

Commitment One: Lead Your Whole Self Well

If you're the one driving your midlife experience, leading yourself well is the first step. But here's the catch: We're often the hardest person to lead. We're great at rationalizing, telling ourselves stories that keep us stuck. Leading yourself well starts with owning your mindset, your growth, and your well-being.

You are the architect of your life. Every choice is a quiet act of design. The foundations you build, the habits you keep, the care you bring to each step—all of it shapes the way you live. Life invites participation, not just reaction. And while challenges are inevitable, resilience is found in grace, in learning, in the quiet return to what matters. Leading yourself is not about control, but about presence. It's a steady practice, shaped in the small, deliberate moments of each day.

You can't just lead the parts of yourself that come easy. Real change happens when you lead your whole self—heart, mind, body, and soul. That's where the power is. That's when things begin to shift.

Commitment Two: Tell Yourself the Truth

There's a quiet, liberating power in being honest with yourself. It's like clearing away the masks you've been wearing. You can finally exhale, letting yourself be fully seen—not perfect, but real. But being honest with yourself is an act of courage. It's standing in the discomfort of your own truth and facing your fears instead of running from them. It's owning your imperfections while still embracing your strengths, understanding they're both part of what makes you whole.

This kind of self-honesty is the starting point for everything that matters. It creates a foundation for growth and transformation. It helps you be kinder to yourself, to hold space for your mistakes without letting them define you. And it opens the door to the kind of deep, meaningful connections we all long for. When you embrace honesty, you create the possibility of a second half of life that feels intentional, authentic, and alive.

Commitment Three: Practice Radical Acceptance

There's strength in learning to see life as it is—the good, the bad, and everything in between. Acceptance means finding a clear and solid foundation in reality so you can move forward with purpose.

Radical acceptance isn't resignation. It's fully owning the moment you're in. It's recognizing that while you can't control everything that happens, you do control how you respond. When you stop resisting reality, you stop wasting energy on what you can't change and start focusing on what you can. That's where real progress happens—when you lead yourself with clarity and resilience, creating a path forward that's grounded in intention.

One of the biggest misconceptions about acceptance is that it means approving of everything, even when we've been wronged. But acceptance doesn't mean condoning injustice or pretending things are okay. It involves recognizing the truth of what's happened so you can process it and move beyond it. Radical acceptance clears the way for growth, healing, and action, allowing you to take the next step with strength and clarity.

Seven Mindset Shifts

Just a few key mindset shifts can transform the way you see and move through the world. The goal is to clear space, refocus on what truly matters, and make deliberate, thoughtful changes that ripple through everything you do.

These seven mindset shifts aren't rules or hacks. They're invitations to step into a way of living that feels more connected, more alive, and more grounded. They're practical, real, and rooted in what research—and life—has shown actually works. These shifts can open doors to a life with more ease, joy, and connection. Let's walk through them together.

Shift into Curiosity:
Release the Shackles of Certainty

Ever find yourself feeling stuck, like you're gripping too tightly to what's familiar? It's something we all go through. We cling to our comfort zones because change can be overwhelming, even scary. But this tight grip can make it hard to move through life's inevitable ups and downs, leaving us stressed and resistant to growth.

What if we approached it differently—not with certainty, but with curiosity? A growth mindset invites us to loosen our grip, to see ourselves not as finished but unfolding. We begin to understand that our abilities, like our lives, are always in motion. With this shift comes a quiet resilience, a softening toward failure, a deeper willingness to learn. Imagine the possibilities that emerge when we stop needing to be right and instead welcome the unknown as a teacher. The path may not be clear, but it is alive.

Shift into Connection:
You Aren't Meant to Do This Alone

What if the key to truly discovering who you are isn't endless introspection but reaching outward, connecting with the people around you? We'll explore the idea that when we stop obsessing over ourselves, we actually uncover more of who we're meant to be. When we shift from what we can get to what we can give, we step into a reality where joy and purpose aren't just abstract concepts. They become the rhythm of our daily lives, embodied in acts of kindness and connection. This goes beyond just feeling better. It's creating a life filled with meaning and a lasting impact.

But here's the tension. Some of us give so much we lose ourselves in the process. If you've been pouring out without pause, it's time to check in. You can't lead others well if you're running on empty. The work is holding both: caring for others and caring for yourself. That's how we sustain a life of depth and impact. That's how we keep showing up whole.

Shift into Response-Ability: The Pause That Changes Things

We have far more control over our emotions than we give ourselves credit for. Life throws challenge our way, and it's easy to feel like we're at the mercy of our feelings, letting frustration, anger, or sadness take the reins. But what if we could harness that control, guiding our emotions rather than being guided by them? We have the power to choose our responses and shape our emotional landscape.

Consider this: When faced with a setback, what if, instead of letting those automatic reactions take over, you paused? What if you gave yourself the space to breathe and decide how you want to feel, how you want to respond? We can approach life's difficulties with a sense of curiosity and openness, turning away from frustration and toward exploration. Imagine the difference it could make to face challenges not with the instinct to complain but with a mindset of curiosity: "What can this situation teach me? How can I grow from this?" This shift in perspective transforms more than how you handle obstacles. It transforms how you experience life itself.

Shift into Alignment: Sync with What Matters

Listen to that still, quiet voice. What stirs your soul? What fills you with energy? What moves you to tears? These questions reveal the meaning already woven into your life, present in each moment. Viktor Frankl, in *Man's Search for Meaning*, drew on Nietzsche's insight: "He who has a *why* to live for can bear almost any *how*." Frankl, a Holocaust survivor, saw in the darkest of places how purpose can sustain a person through anything. That deeper "why" steadies you, guides you through the highs and lows, and keeps you grounded in what truly matters.

While it's important to seek meaning, it's just as crucial to acknowledge the meaning that's already woven into your life. It's so easy to get caught up in the hustle, always looking for that next big thing, that next profound moment of purpose. But what if you paused and recognized the meaning that's already here? Sometimes, in our relentless pursuit of more, we miss the beauty right in front of us. By listening to your inner voice and aligning with your passions, you're not just chasing after meaning; you're living it, here and now. And when you do that, your life bursts with purpose, authenticity, and joy.

Shift into Befriending Your Body:
The Companion That's Brought You Here

Your body has been with you through everything—every joy, every heartbreak, every single moment of your life. But how often do you stop to truly care for it, to thank it, to honor it? As Jim Rohn said, "Take care of your body. It's the only place you have to live." In midlife, your body has new opinions. This shift is about building a relationship with your body based on listening, care, and respect.

What does that look like? Nourishing it with food that fuels you. Moving in ways that make you feel alive. Giving it the rest it deserves. When you care for your body, it shows up for you—with energy, strength, and resilience. Your body is your lifelong companion. Befriend it. Care for it. And watch how it supports you in ways you never imagined.

Shift into Stillness:
The World Won't Stop, but You Can

This shift is leaning in. Seeing clearly. Stepping forward with courage. Stillness is a way to ground yourself, to find strength amid life's complexities, and to meet them with resilience and compassion. We'll explore stillness as a sanctuary, a space to tune into your life and uncover what it truly means to live well. Moments of quiet reflection are opportunities for deeper self-awareness, emotional strength, and genuine connection with others.

Drawing from my own journey and the insights of others, we'll look at simple ways to bring stillness into your everyday life—through solitude, nature, or mindfulness. You'll come to see stillness as more than a pause.

Your second half isn't about playing it safe; **it's about playing it real.**

———

It's renewal. It's a chance to live from a place of integrity and alignment.

Shift into Brave: Cultivate the Courage to Shift

Change is the crossroads where comfort meets possibility (a place both terrifying and exhilarating) where you decide what comes next. Whether it's a quiet nudge or a loud wake-up call, the need for change often signals the start of something new. We'll look at how to recognize when it's time to let go of what's no longer working, how to trust the quiet whispers guiding you toward something better, and how to face fear without letting it hold you back. Change isn't easy, but it's where growth lives. It's where you step out of the familiar and into a life that feels more aligned, more true, more fully alive.

This is an invitation to take that first step. To listen. To trust. To embrace the uncertainty and the possibility that comes with it. Let's start there.

How to Get the Most Out of Reading This Book (Or Anything, Really)

This book is designed to be a simple read, but there are several ways you can deepen your engagement and make the most of it.

Reflect and journal: Even though it's an easy read, take your time with it. Read in sections and pause to reflect after each one. Each chapter contains Pause & Reflect questions; you'll see them throughout. Keep a journal nearby and jot down your thoughts and insights. This reflection is where much of the magic happens.

Read with a friend: Grab your partner or a friend and read the book together. Discuss it over coffee, a walk, or even a video call. What's bubbling up for you? How are the insights and questions resonating with each of you? These conversations can deepen your understanding and provide new perspectives.

Explore the science: If you're a science enthusiast, I've got you covered. I've created a website for *Shift* that highlights the studies and references supporting the topics discussed in the book (www.shiftintomidlife.com). It's all sorted by chapter, providing an easy way to dive deeper into the research behind the concepts.

Create a reading ritual: Consider reading at the same time every day. Establishing a routine can be powerful. If your mornings are open, start your day with some reading. Your brain is fresh and ready to absorb new information, setting a reflective tone for the day. If your mornings are chaotic, make it part of your evening ritual. Wind down by reflecting on the day's challenges and insights, giving you meaningful thoughts to ponder as you drift off to sleep.

Join one of our coaching circles: Dive deeper by joining one of our book clubs at InHabit.Life (www.inhabit.life). Connect with others who are on the same journey, share insights, and gain new perspectives in a supportive community.

Join the 30-day journaling challenge: When you finish the book, don't stop there! Visit InHabit.Life and download "Intermission," my 30-day journaling challenge, designed to help you continue the journey of reflection and personal growth.

Welcome to Your Second Half: A Different Kind of Becoming

This book isn't about changing who you are. It will guide you on a journey of rediscovering who you already are. It's about recognizing your strengths and experiences, embracing who you are becoming, and stepping into the next chapter with confidence and purpose. It means focusing on what aging adds to your life, not what it takes away. My hope is that this book provides clarity and practical encouragement, a space to think on what really matters as you move forward. There are no quick fixes. It's going to take practical, meaningful shifts in how you think and live. Together, we'll navigate what it looks like to live intentionally, to lean into the challenges and opportunities, and to write the best chapters of your story yet. Let's get to work.

PART ONE

PREPARING TO SHIFT

BEFORE WE GO ANYWHERE, we start here, with you. With the life you've lived so far. The story that brought you to this page. Not the polished version, but the real one. The one with moments you're proud of and moments you'd rather forget. The one with love and loss, clarity and confusion, trying and trying again.

This part is about paying attention, taking a breath, and naming what's true. You don't need to have it all figured out. You just need to be willing to look. Because before we roll up our sleeves and do the work ahead, we begin with the most important thing you bring to this whole journey—yourself.

1
LIFE IN TWO HALVES
THE ART OF BECOMING

Packing Light

I used to travel with trunks,
leather-strapped, brass-cornered,
each one bulging
with trophies from younger days—
ambition, opinion,
a fondness for being right.
I lugged them through my thirties,
wheeled them into forties,
and by fifty,
I was starting to wonder
if maybe I didn't need
three variations of the same self.
So I started unpacking.
Not all at once—
just a few grudges here,

a should or two there.
That one awkward memory
I kept under a sweater
from the '90s—gone.
It's not that I'm empty now.
Just... lighter.
Able to notice
the birds again.
To say, "I don't know,"
without checking the mirror.
To read poetry
without looking for the point.
The second half,
I've discovered,
isn't about adding more—
but knowing what to leave behind
so you can carry
a thermos of tea,
a notebook,
and both hands free.

A New Way of Seeing Life

At some point, we find ourselves standing at the edge of life's second half with a quieter kind of readiness. The kind that comes from having carried enough, for long enough, to finally ask, "What can I set down?"

The bags aren't as heavy as they once were, but they're still full. Expectations. Assumptions. Outdated maps of who we're supposed to be. And then, one day, we begin to unpack a little at a time. A belief that no longer fits. A version of ourselves we no longer need to protect. A memory that's done its work.

And as we sort through it all, we begin to see that the road here has shaped us, every stretch of it. The seasons of striving. The years of holding it all together. The losses, the loves, the lessons we never saw coming. It's all in us now, woven into who we are. Most of it strengthens us. Some of it asks to be released.

This is where the second half begins.

Not with a blaze of glory, but with a deep breath. A lighter step. A willingness to let go of what no longer serves us, so we can travel with intention. Hands free. Heart open. Room made for what matters now. The road ahead isn't about becoming someone entirely new. It's about becoming more you. Clearer. Kinder. Less burdened by the weight of proving, and more alive to the wonder of simply being.

I first encountered the concept of life in two halves during a New Year's road trip with my wife, Jodi, to Cannon Beach, Oregon, a place that holds a special place in our hearts. We have a tradition of stopping by Trader Joe's for some of our favorite treats: apricot Stilton, cookie butter, and everything-but-the-bagel seasoning. On that trip, we had something particularly meaningful to accompany us: the audiobook of Richard Rohr's *Falling Upward: A Spirituality for the Two Halves of Life*, which had been highly recommended by a trusted friend and colleague.

As soon as we hit play, we were hooked. The seven-hour trip flew by as we listened, discussed, and absorbed the book's profound insights. Both of us, just a year into our fifties, were keenly aware that we were likely past life's midpoint—a realization that was both comforting and a bit uncomfortable.

Shifting from Social to Spiritual

The first half of life is a social journey—a quest for identity. We're busy going to school, building careers, growing networks, and starting families. It's a whirlwind of activity and ambition, influenced heavily by our upbringing, teachers, and society. We're in a massive learning lab, figuring out who we are and how we fit into the world.

But then something shifts. The second half of life invites us to go deeper, to move beyond the social constructs and external validations. Climbing the ladder matters less than uncovering true purpose. We start asking bigger questions: "What truly matters to me?" "What gives my life meaning?" This is where the spiritual journey kicks in, inviting us to reconcile our past experiences, embrace our inner wisdom, and align our lives with our deeper values.

Letting Go of Old Scripts

Carl Jung captured this transition perfectly when he wrote, "We cannot live the afternoon of life according to the program of life's morning; for what was great in the morning will be little at evening, and what in the morning was true will at evening have become a lie." The rules and goals that guided us in the first half of our lives don't necessarily apply in the second half.

In the morning of life, we're building: careers, families, identities. We're driven by external measures of success and validation. But as we move into the afternoon, we realize that what once seemed so crucial might not hold the same weight anymore. It's a shift from striving to being, from external approval to internal fulfillment.

Embracing Paradox

As we step into the second half of life, something remarkable happens. We start to understand, absorb, and reconcile all the experiences we've gathered along the way. It's like looking at a puzzle that's finally coming together, each piece revealing a clearer picture of who we are and where we're headed.

James Hollis, in his book *Finding Meaning in the Second Half of Life*, nails it when he says that our focus shifts dramatically as we age. In the first half, we're driven by the question, "What is the world asking of me?" We chase success, approval, and all those external markers of achievement.

But then comes the pivot. The second half of life invites a more profound question: "What is my soul asking of me?" This isn't just a subtle shift; it's a seismic one. We start to move away from rigid rules and embrace principles, learning to hold seemingly opposite concepts in tension. We realize we can be both objective and optimistic, future-minded and present, confident and humble, slow-thinking and fast-acting, introspective and outward-focused, careful and courageous. And yes, we can experience pain and joy simultaneously.

Paradox lives in the space between; it's the stretch and tension, the push and pull that we learn to live with, not solve. Holding two truths at once—like light and shadow, gain and loss, or hope and fear—opens up something rare. It asks us to let go of certainty and settle into the complexity. And maybe that's the point: If we're able to hold both, to see from both sides, we've crossed over to something richer, something more grounded and whole. It's the quiet mark of wisdom, landing on the other shore.

Navigating the Second Half with Grace

The beauty of this stage is that it allows us to lead more authentic and fulfilling lives. We become masters at navigating life's paradoxes, seeing that our greatest strengths often emerge from our greatest vulnerabilities. This journey of self-discovery and acceptance enriches the second half of life, turning it into a time of profound meaning and purpose.

The second half can feel intimidating because it often lacks the structure of the first, leaving us to figure it out on our own. Without that clarity, we can find ourselves

Paradox is the quiet mark of wisdom: learning to live in the stretch between what was and what's next.

———————

clinging to first-half behaviors, delaying the transition to second-half thinking. These behaviors might include chasing external validation through career achievements or material possessions and focusing on accumulating more—whether wealth, accolades, or experiences—in a frantic attempt to fill existential voids. This "failure to launch" can result in what's commonly known as a midlife crisis, manifesting as an anxious pursuit to achieve or acquire more, even when those pursuits no longer align with deeper values. Carl Jung is often quoted as saying the first half of life is devoted to forming a healthy ego; the second half is going inward and letting go of it. While the exact source is debated, the truth it points to resonates. The first half is all about building—identity; achievement; a place in the world. But the second half invites a different kind of work. It calls us inward. It asks us to loosen our grip on the self we've so carefully constructed and begin the gentler, braver process of release. Our focus shifts from crisis to opportunity. It's a chance to refocus, redefine, and realign our lives with our deeper, more spiritual aspirations.

Embracing the Wisdom of Age

Embracing midlife is recognizing and seizing the opportunity that comes with age. It's shifting from a mindset of acquisition and achievement to one of meaning and purpose. As we navigate this journey, we can find peace in the transition, knowing our experiences have equipped us with the wisdom to live more authentically and purposefully.

The second half of life provides us with the opportunity to leverage the hindsight of the first. We can step more deeply and confidently into who we are and focus on the relationships and pursuits that are most important to us. We can also let go of those things that have kept us from doing so.

I'm thankful for the friend who recommended *Falling Upward* to us. The work it inspired has been invigorating and life-giving. It has led me to some of my most important life and career decisions. First, I had to acknowledge that no one was coming to do that work for me and it likely wouldn't happen by accident (although sometimes life has a funny way of catching our attention). My hope is your interest may be likewise ignited to explore the opportunities that await you in your second half. I believe that with intention and the benefit of hindsight, your second half can be richer than your first. Your best years are not behind you—they await you.

TL;DR

- The second half of life isn't just focused on achievement; it's also focused on depth, meaning, and living "forward."

- This phase shifts from doing to becoming, letting go of old roles and stepping into something freer, truer.

- Midlife is full of paradox—joy and sorrow, movement and stillness—and learning to hold both brings wisdom and authenticity.

- This season offers a new kind of freedom in the chance to focus on what truly matters: relationships, self-discovery, and purpose.

- When we step into this shift with intention, our experiences become our guide, leading us toward a life that feels rich, grounded, and fully alive.

PAUSE & REFLECT

- What shaped the way you see the world? Family, faith, culture—where have they given you a solid foundation, and where have they set limits?

- Are you living your life, or just the life expected of you? If you peeled back the layers—expectations, obligations, all the "shoulds"—what would remain? And what would it look like to step fully into *that* story?

- What happens when you really listen—to yourself? When things feel "fine" but not quite right, what's underneath that? A restlessness? A quiet knowing? What might change if you paid attention?
- What shifts when you view midlife as an opportunity versus a challenge?

2
MINDSET AND MIDLIFE
THE LENS THAT CHANGES EVERYTHING

SPOILER ALERT: Your mindset determines your midlife experience. So it's worth getting a handle on it before it gets a handle on you.

We hear the term "mindset" tossed around constantly, like confetti at the Super Bowl. It's everywhere, fluttering down in bits and pieces. But does anyone really know what it means? On the surface, it sounds simple—just the way you think, right? But dig a little deeper and you'll find that mindset is more like a never-ending renovation project in an old house. You think you just need to paint the walls, but suddenly you're tearing down sheetrock and rewiring the whole place.

Mindset is the underlying force that drives your actions, decisions, and how you respond when things don't go according to plan. It's the framework that shapes how you see the world and your place in it. It's the lens through which you view and interpret everything around you. Work on your mindset, and it can be the foundation of something great. Ignore it, and you'll end up wondering why things aren't working out the way you hoped.

Neuroplasticity and Mindset

And let's not forget about the power of neuroplasticity—the brain's remarkable ability to change and adapt at any age. This concept reinforces the power of a growth mindset. It's a reminder that we're never too old to learn, evolve, and become the person we've always wanted to be. A mindset rooted in neuroplasticity says, "I can change my brain, and in doing so, I can change my life." It's understanding that our thoughts, behaviors, and habits are malleable, and with intention, we can shape them in ways that serve our highest goals.

The Midlife Mindset Map

Midlife is a time of reckoning—a phase when we start to question the stories we've been telling ourselves about who we are and what we're capable of. It's a pivotal moment when we're called to reassess, redefine, and reimagine our lives. How we navigate this time depends heavily on our mindset. That's where the Midlife Mindset

Map comes in. It's a framework designed to help you identify and, when necessary, shift your mindset to move through midlife with clarity, purpose, and intention.

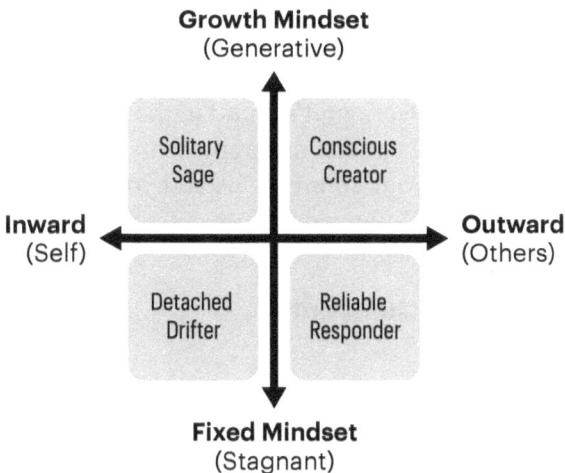

The map has two dimensions: growth versus fixed and inward versus outward. These are the lenses through which we view our lives, determining whether midlife is a time of thriving or merely surviving.

Growth versus fixed mindset: Carol Dweck's work shows us a simple truth: A growth mindset is the belief that we're not finished yet. It's leaning into challenges, treating effort like an old friend, and turning setbacks into stepping stones. A fixed mindset? That's the belief that who you are today is all you'll ever be. The Midlife Mindset Map dares you to ask, "Where am I stuck, and how can I shift toward possibility?"

Inward versus outward mindset: Looking inward is a beautiful thing. A deep, quiet journey. But stay there too long and it can turn into isolation. The outward mindset says, "Look up. Look out. Connect." Because life isn't just found in reflection; it's found in the giving, the sharing, the showing up. The map represents both your inner world shaping your connections and your connections lighting up your inner world.

Exploring the Quadrants

The intersection of these axes creates four key mindsets within the Midlife Mindset Map. Let's explore each one in depth, along with the strengths, challenges, and opportunities for growth they present.

Detached Drifter

The Detached Drifter has retreated from fully engaging with life. Maybe you were once on a path of growth, but somewhere along the way, you stalled. Now, you find yourself content to watch from the sidelines, wrapped in the illusion of comfort. But here's the hard truth: When you're a Detached Drifter, you're not truly living. The pitfall here is a lack of agency—you lose the ability to steer your own life. This can be a dangerous place, where potential withers and resignation quietly takes root.

Imagine Jane, who once had big dreams of starting her own business but now finds herself simply going through the motions at her current job. She's comfortable but unfulfilled. Recognizing her Detached Drifter mindset was the first step toward reigniting her passion and taking small steps toward her entrepreneurial goals.

Reliable Responder

The Reliable Responder has made a life out of giving—always there when someone needs them, tying their self-worth to how much they can serve others. While there's a beautiful nobility in this, the danger is self-forgetting. You become so focused on others that you neglect your own needs, leading to burnout. The challenge for the Reliable Responder is to set boundaries, practice self-care, and remember that you can't pour from an empty cup.

Consider Mark, who spent years being the go-to person for his family, friends, and colleagues. It wasn't until he faced a health crisis that he realized he had been neglecting his own well-being. Learning to say no and prioritizing self-care became essential for him to continue being there for others without losing himself.

Solitary Sage

The Solitary Sage is the introspective explorer, diving deep into self-reflection and personal growth. This is where wisdom is born, but there's a risk of loneliness—becoming so absorbed in your inner world that you disconnect from the relationships and experiences that

Change your mindset, and **you change your midlife.**

———————

make life meaningful. The challenge for the Solitary Sage is to balance introspection with connection, sharing your wisdom with others and staying engaged with the world.

Think of Maya, who spent years in meditation and self-study, gaining incredible insights but feeling increasingly isolated. By engaging a coach and joining a book club to engage in meaningful conversations, she found a way to share her wisdom and build connections that enriched her life.

Conscious Creator

Finally, we have the Conscious Creator—someone deeply engaged with both their inner world and the world around them. Conscious Creators live at the intersection of personal growth and community impact. They're not just focused on their own journey; they're actively contributing to the lives of others. The challenge here is being present—staying grounded in the moment while pursuing future goals.

Consider Alex, who launched a community project to support local entrepreneurs. While passionate about his work, he realized he was missing out on everyday moments with his family. By practicing mindfulness, he learned to be present at home while continuing to drive his project forward.

The Journey Forward

The Midlife Mindset Map is your guide through the evolving terrain of midlife. It's a way to check in with yourself, to understand your current mindset, and to make conscious choices about where you want to go next. Midlife isn't a crisis—it's an opportunity. It's your chance to redefine, reimagine, and create a life that's as rich and layered as you are.

So, where are you on this map? And more importantly, where do you want to be? Start today: Choose one mindset you'd like to shift, and take a small, meaningful action toward that change. Because every step you take shapes the life you're creating, and the journey of midlife is one of ongoing growth, connection, and fulfillment.

The Midlife Mindset Map is a crucial part of the equation, but it's just one piece of a much larger puzzle. As you navigate the twists and turns of midlife, other mindsets also play an essential role in shaping your journey. Let's explore some of these and how they can either hold you back or propel you forward into the life you truly want to live.

Subtracting Versus Adding

Okay, let's talk about how you view aging itself. A subtractive mindset sees aging as a process of loss. Every year, something slips away—your energy, your opportunities, your relevance. It's easy to get caught up in this narrative, to feel like life is slowly being chipped away from you. "It's all downhill from here!" But what if we flipped the script? An additive mindset looks at aging as a process of gaining. With time comes wisdom, experience, and perspective—plus new opportunities, fewer time constraints, expanded networks, refined skills, and other practical advantages. This mindset turns midlife from something to dread into something to embrace. It's seeing your life not as something that's shrinking, but as something that's expanding.

Abundance Versus Scarcity

Then there's the way you view the world's resources—be it love, success, or happiness. A scarcity mindset is driven by fear and the belief that these resources are limited, so if someone else gets more, you get less. This mindset breeds competition, hoarding, and a sense of never having enough. On the other hand, an abundance mindset sees the world as full of possibilities. It's believing there's more than enough to go around, fostering generosity and open-hearted living. With an abundance mindset, you're thriving because you're tapping into the infinite possibilities life has to offer. You're happy to give things away, knowing that they'll come back and others will do the same for you.

Resilience and Mindset

Challenges are inevitable, especially in midlife. How you respond to these challenges defines who you are. Resilience isn't simply bouncing back; it's bouncing forward, turning setbacks into a springboard for growth. A resilient mindset keeps you moving, even when the road is bumpy and you're not sure what's around the next bend. It's the belief that no matter what happens, you have the strength not only to endure but to emerge stronger and more determined than before.

So here you are—with the Midlife Mindset Map and a toolkit of powerful mindsets to explore. The road ahead is yours to navigate, and the good news is that you're in control. Mindset is dynamic and changeable; you have the power to shape it. As we continue this journey together, we'll dive into practical steps for making these mindset shifts and intentionally designing a life that reflects your deepest values. The work you do on your mindset will ripple out into every area of your life, transforming both how you see the world and how you move through it.

TL;DR

- Mindset is everything. It shapes how you experience midlife—how you see challenges, relationships, and what's possible next.

- The Midlife Mindset Map lays out four ways we navigate this season: Detached Drifter, Reliable Responder, Solitary Sage, and Conscious Creator. Each has a pull; each has a possibility.

- A growth mindset isn't just optimism; it's recognizing that we're not done yet. That we can keep learning, shifting, evolving. There's a tension here: between looking inward for clarity and reaching outward for connection. One without the other keeps us stuck.

- Aging isn't subtraction; it's addition. More wisdom. More experience. More depth. What if this stage of life was about expansion, not decline? Resilience isn't just bouncing back; it's bouncing forward. Taking what life throws at you and turning it into something new.

- The invitation is clear: Step into this season with intention. Your mindset isn't fixed, your story isn't finished, and the life you want is still being written.

PAUSE & REFLECT

- Where do you find yourself on the Midlife Mindset Map, and what's calling you to move, shift, and evolve?

- If you move toward a growth mindset, how might that change the way you see the challenges right in front of you?

- What assumptions have you made about midlife? And are they based on evidence or outdated narratives?

- How do you balance time spent looking inward with time spent engaging outward? Where do you tend to lean, and what might need adjusting?

- How often do you challenge your own thinking? If you had to argue against your own limiting beliefs, what evidence would you present?

3

THE SECOND-HALF ADVANTAGE
THE VIEW FROM "OVER THE HILL"

THERE COMES A MOMENT when you realize the path you've been walking isn't the whole story. It's like reaching the summit of a long, steep hill and finally pausing to catch your breath. You look back at the winding trails, the sheer effort it took to get here, and you see how far you've come. You're not the same person who started this climb.

My friend Chip Conley says that being "over the hill" gets a bad rap. The term showed up in the 1950s and got picked up by Hallmark to sell cheeky birthday cards, turning fifty into a punchline. But let's rethink that for a second. From the top of the hill, the view is better. The air is clearer. And the hike gets easier. You're no longer pushing relentlessly upward, lungs burning, legs aching. Instead, there's a kind of momentum—a grace—to the journey forward. Saying that, you do have to be mindful of your knees on the descent.

The first half of life? It's a scramble. It's about collecting: experiences, knowledge, achievements. You're piecing together an identity from what you do, the roles you play, and the milestones you check off. You think if you can just add enough, the puzzle will come together, and suddenly you'll know who you are.

But then something shifts.

You start to see that the identity you've built, while important, isn't the whole story. It's a chapter, not an entire book. And perhaps most freing of all: It doesn't have to continue to define you. And here's the beautiful, unexpected gift of the second half: It's the chance to take a step back and see your life with fresh eyes.

It's no longer about climbing for the sake of climbing. It's about curating. You begin to ask different questions: "What do I want to carry with me? What can I let go of? What truly matters?" The experiences you've had and the lessons you've learned become your guide. With that clarity, you stop reacting to life and start leading it.

But leading doesn't mean holding on tighter. In fact, it's the opposite. It's letting go. Letting go of outdated roles, distractions, and the noise that no longer seems to matter. By clearing away the clutter, you make space for what's real—for what brings you joy, fulfillment, and meaning.

Enter Identity

In the lead-up to selling my business and making the leap into a master's program in positive psychology, aging, and midlife transitions, I found myself asking some big questions. Who am I when I'm no longer defined by this work? What comes next? And how do I even begin to figure that out? As part of my journey, I attended a workshop with Renovaré, an organization focused on spiritual formation and helping people build deeper, more intentional connections with God and themselves. One session on identity completely shifted my perspective. The facilitator challenged us to stop thinking of identity as something you have to hunt for—something external that you find and hold onto. Instead, they asked us to step into it. To claim it. To move from searching to deciding who you want to be and what kind of life you want to live.

For me, this was a game-changing moment. It reframed identity not as a fixed destination but as a choice—a dynamic process of becoming. It helped me let go of the relentless pursuit of "finding myself" and instead focus on intentionally shaping the next chapter of my life. It wasn't just a profound spiritual insight; it was a practical strategy for growth and change. And it was exactly what I needed to move forward.

Enter Laughing

The second half of life invites us to hold it all a little more loosely. To laugh at the mess, the missteps, and even ourselves, because laughter is what keeps us human. It breaks the tension, softens the sharp edges, and reminds us that perfection was never the destination. Growth is. And when we learn to laugh along the way, we realize that maybe growing was always meant to feel a little lighter.

This isn't ignoring the hard stuff. It's naming it, feeling it, but not letting it take over. Shifting the weight just enough to keep moving. Because even in the thick of it, laughter brings freedom—a reminder the story isn't over, and the next step is yours.

Enter Courage

The second half of life asks for a different kind of bravery. Not the loud, chest-pounding kind, but a quiet, grounded courage. The kind that whispers, "Let go." Let go of what no longer fits, what you've outgrown, what's been holding you back. It's the courage to take risks—not reckless leaps, but intentional steps that align with the person you're becoming. To trust that, even in uncertainty, you already carry everything you need to step into what's next. Because you do.

This is your second-half advantage. Rather than racing to the next summit or checking off a list, you're savoring the view, curating a life that feels true, and stepping boldly into the unknown, carried by the wisdom you've gathered along the way.

Decoding Life Satisfaction

In the second half of life, things start to shift. The road ahead feels narrower, more focused. But the sky above you opens wide. The pace of earlier years finally slows, giving you a chance to breathe, to look around, and to notice. You stop sprinting and start walking. In that walking, you discover a deeper rhythm, one grounded in the stories you've lived and the lessons they've left behind.

What fascinates me about this stage of life is how much we actually know about it. The research is overflowing with clues—practical, powerful ideas about what makes the second half strong. My curiosity with midlife has turned into a kind of obsession, and the more I dive into the data, the more I see that this isn't a time to coast or drift. It's a time to grow, thrive, and live with intention.

So what have we learned? What are the key insights that can help you create a stronger, richer, more meaningful midlife? Here are seven findings to guide the way.

How You See Aging Matters

Your perspective on aging shapes everything. If you see this stage of life as decline, it can become a weight you carry. But if you see it as growth—an unfolding of wisdom and possibility—it transforms the way you live. The research is clear: People who cultivate a positive view of aging and recognize there is still so much ahead consistently report higher satisfaction.

Relationships Are the Core
At the heart of a fulfilling life are the people we walk it with: family, friends, community. These connections aren't just nice to have; they're essential. They're where we find belonging, strength, and joy. When those connections are missing, the research tells us that loneliness can creep in, affecting not just our happiness but also our health. If you're going to invest in anything, invest in the relationships that matter most.

Purpose Fuels Everything
Having a sense of purpose is like having a compass. It gives you direction, clarity, and the motivation to keep moving forward. Purpose doesn't have to be grand or world-changing. It's found in the ways you show up, contribute, and live with meaning. Whether it's through your work, your family, or a cause you believe in, purpose is the thing that gets you up in the morning and keeps you going, even on the hard days.

Befriend Your Body
Let's talk about your body. Not as something to conquer or whip into shape, but as a partner. A friend. In the first half of life, it's easy to push your body too hard, to ignore its needs, or to treat it as an afterthought. But midlife invites us to shift that relationship. The research shows that taking care of your body—through movement,

The second half of life calls for a quieter kind of courage: **the courage to let go.**

---

nourishing food, and rest—is deeply tied to how you feel mentally and emotionally. Befriending your body means listening to it, respecting it, and giving it what it needs to thrive. When you do, it pays you back in energy, clarity, and joy.

Emotional Resilience Is Key

Life doesn't stop being messy. There are still twists and turns, highs and lows. But the way you handle those moments? That's what makes the difference. Emotional resilience isn't pretending everything is fine; it's learning how to stay grounded when it's not. Practices like mindfulness, gratitude, and leaning on your support system can help you navigate the storms. You'll still feel the waves, but resilience means you've learned how to ride them.

Embrace Change and Stay Open

Midlife is full of transitions. Kids grow up. Careers shift. Life looks different than you thought it would. But here's the thing: Change isn't the enemy. It's the teacher. People who embrace change and stay curious and open to new experiences thrive in the second half of life. A growth mindset—the belief that challenges are opportunities to learn—can transform how you navigate transitions. Instead of resisting the twists and turns, you lean into them. And in that leaning, you grow.

Celebrate the Small Wins

We often think accomplishment is about the big stuff—the promotions, the awards, the milestones. But midlife teaches us to pay attention to the small wins and the everyday moments that matter. It might be finishing a project you've been putting off, reconnecting with an old friend, or simply pausing to appreciate a quiet morning. Research shows that celebrating these small victories leads to greater satisfaction. Because life isn't a checklist. It's those moments that stop you in your tracks, the ones that whisper, *Yes, this is good. This matters.*

The Power of Promises

There's one more piece to the puzzle: the promises you make and keep, both to others and to yourself. When you say, "I'm going to do this," and you follow through, you're building trust with yourself as well as with others. Over time, this self-trust becomes a kind of quiet strength. It's what allows you to face uncertainty with confidence, knowing you're aligned with what's real and true. It's what keeps you steady when everything else feels unsteady.

I THINK OF THIS STAGE of life as a kind of clearing. Not the dramatic fork in the road we're told to expect, but something quieter. A moment where you can see more clearly—what's working, what's not, and what's asking to change.

These seven findings are ones I've tested in my own life and in conversation with others walking similar paths, and they're reinforced by science. Research backs what experience has already whispered: We can shape a more grounded, meaningful, and satisfying life from here.

So take a breath. Look around. Let yourself feel the weight of how far you've come, and the quiet possibility of what still lies ahead. And then ask yourself the question I keep returning to: What's ready to grow now?

TL;DR

- Midlife brings clarity. It's the pause that invites you to take stock, reflect, realign, and move forward with intention. Less grind, more meaning.

- You're not over the hill; you're on top of it. The view is wider. The air is clearer. And if you let it, momentum will carry you forward.

- The first half focused on gathering—titles, possessions, achievements. The second shifts to refining. What truly matters? Keep that. Let the rest go.

- Own your identity. You don't have to keep searching for who you're supposed to be. You get to decide. Step into it. Live it fully.

- Courage isn't always found in pushing forward. Sometimes, it lies in letting go of what no longer fits and trusting what comes next.

- Relationships matter most. At the end of the day, it's not what you built but who you built it with. The people who walk with you—invest in them.
- Small wins keep you moving. It's not about the big leaps. It's the small, steady steps and the quiet shifts. Pay attention. Celebrate them.

PAUSE & REFLECT

- How do you really feel about aging? What if you started viewing it as a time of growth, a time to open up to what's possible?
- Who are the people in your life who truly lift you up, and how are you showing up for them in return?
- What genuinely fills you with a sense of meaning? How can you bring more of that into your everyday?
- How do your daily actions reflect what matters most to you? And if they do not, what's one shift you could make to live closer to your core?

4

LOOKING INWARD TO LOOK OUTWARD

MIDLIFE INVITES US to stop and pay attention—to pause the relentless striving and turn inward, asking the questions we've avoided for too long. Who am I now? Beneath the roles I've played, the labels I've worn, and the expectations I've carried, what's left at the core? This is not dwelling on the past or staying trapped in old stories. It is clarity, the slow and patient work of peeling back layers to reveal the truths that have been there all along, quietly waiting to be seen. These truths remind us of who we have always been and invite us to step into who we are becoming. When we look honestly at what is stirring beneath the surface, we uncover the values, beliefs, and strengths that hold our lives together. From that place of clarity, we move forward with intention.

Here's the question: What stories are you still carrying? The ones that shaped you, the ones you've outgrown, and the ones that no longer serve but still take up space. The more we name them, the more we understand ourselves. And the more we understand ourselves, the more fully we show up with clarity, with courage, and with a heart ready for what's next.

The Stories We Carry

We are walking collections of stories—some spoken, some unspoken. These stories shape how we see the world, how we see ourselves, and how we move through life. Some stories lift us up. Others weigh us down. Some are so loud we can't ignore them, while others lie hidden, quietly influencing everything we do.

If we're going to grow, we have to get curious about these stories. Where did they come from? Which ones still serve us? Which ones are long overdue for revision? No judgment, just awareness. It's getting honest so we can step more fully into who we are becoming.

Tools for Clarity and Growth

Turning inward isn't easy. It takes courage—and it takes time and resources. Think of these tools as flashlights, helping illuminate what's been in the shadows. They help us navigate self-discovery with clarity and intention.

The Power of Therapy

When I held focus groups for this book and my research, one thing kept coming up: therapy. Again and again, people named it as the most powerful tool for personal growth. It shines a light on the patterns we keep repeating, helps us make sense of where we've been, and gives us the space to lay down what has been too heavy to carry. And in that space, something new begins to emerge.

Coaching: A Guide for the Future

Coaching opens another door. If therapy helps make sense of where you have been, coaching helps shape where you are going. It is like walking alongside a guide, someone who nudges you to think differently, asks the questions you did not know you needed, and helps you turn insight into action. Coaching doesn't just hand you a roadmap. It helps you get clear on what truly matters and create a life that feels like your own.

Assessments: Unlocking Self-Awareness

Some people swear by assessments. Others dismiss them as simplistic. The truth? They're tools—nothing more, nothing less. Used well, they set you free rather than box you in. When done right, assessments highlight patterns, strengths, and blind spots that might otherwise go unnoticed. Tools like the Big Five, CliftonStrengths, and Emotional Intelligence assessments can provide valuable insights into how you think, connect, and lead. One assessment I highly recommend is the iEQ9 Enneagram (scan the QR code to link to it). Unlike many personality frameworks, it goes beyond behaviors, uncovering core motivations and deeper patterns.

Practicing Mindfulness

Mindfulness is more than stillness. It is movement, breath, and awareness. It is paying attention while walking, drinking your morning coffee, or listening to a friend. It is noticing what rises within you without rushing to judge or fix. It is creating space between reaction and response. The more we tune in, the more we see what is real, what is possible, and what has been waiting for us all along.

Journaling: Making Sense of It All

Journaling helps make sense of it all. Many people love the idea of it but struggle with the practice. They sit down, pen in hand, and suddenly nothing. The blinking cursor. The blank page. Silence. Some worry they are doing it wrong. Others feel self-conscious, like their words need to be profound. Some do not know where to start or have too many thoughts, too much noise, or maybe nothing at all.

Journaling is more than writing the right words. It is writing, period. It is giving yourself permission to be messy, honest, and unfiltered. Some days, it is a flood of thoughts. Other days, a single sentence. And sometimes, it is just showing up, pen to paper, and seeing what unfolds.

From Self-Discovery to Connection

The more we understand ourselves, the more fully we show up for others. In *The Book of Joy*, the Dalai Lama offers a simple but powerful truth: "If you want others to be happy, practice compassion. If you want to be happy, practice compassion." It's a reminder that joy is something we cultivate—through connection, generosity, and showing up for others. The book, co-authored with Archbishop Desmond Tutu, is a beautiful exploration of how meaning, laughter, and love can live alongside pain. It's well worth a read.

Happiness is not found in chasing more—more success, more stuff, more status. Happiness turns outward. Arthur Brooks calls it the second curve of happiness. The first curve is achievement, hustle, and the pursuit of the next big thing. The second is contribution, meaning, and a shift toward others. At some point, the question changes. Instead of asking, "What can I get?" we start asking, "What can I give?" And something opens. The deepest fulfillment is found in the connections we build, the ways we show up, and the moments we give ourselves away.

Growth Moves in Both Directions

Looking inward and looking outward are not separate paths. They're part of the same journey. The more we reflect, the more we see what we have to give. And the more we give, the more we learn about who we are.

So yes—turn inward. Ask the hard questions. Sit with what's uncomfortable. Use the tools that stretch you, shape you, and grow you. But don't stop there. Take what you've uncovered and bring it outward—to connect, contribute, and create.

Midlife is not the place to get stuck in your own head. It is the place to take what you have learned and live it. You're not just asking, "Who am I?" but also, "Who am I becoming?" and "How can I take what I've found and make the world a little better along the way?"

TL;DR

- "Look in so you can look out" is an invitation to reflect deeply on your life, mining the stories of your past to gain clarity for the future.

- Tools like therapy, coaching, mindfulness, and journaling help us uncover our true selves and understand our motivations.

- This self-awareness isn't just for personal growth. It allows us to connect more meaningfully with others and contribute to something greater than ourselves.

- True fulfillment lies in balancing introspection with outward action—knowing ourselves deeply so we can make a real impact on those around us.

PAUSE & REFLECT

- What stories from your past still have lessons to teach you? How might they shape where you're headed?
- How could practices like therapy or journaling help you see yourself more clearly and bring new insights to light?
- Who or what in your life calls out for deeper connection, something that aligns with what really matters to you?
- How could both solitude and connection help you live with greater depth, purpose, and impact?

5

NAVIGATING MIDLIFE'S DERAILERS
OWNING THE PLOT TWISTS

THERE COMES A MOMENT in midlife when things come into focus. It doesn't always happen suddenly. Sometimes, it's a slow unraveling, a quiet sense that something isn't quite right. Other times, it arrives with force, triggered by a health scare, a career shift, or an unexpected loss. Either way, midlife hands you an invitation to stop, pay attention, and look around. Because the things that got you here may not be the things that will take you forward.

When we pause long enough, we start to notice patterns. There are forces that shape our experience, our energy, and our ability to move freely through life. Health. Money. Connection. The Big Three—often referenced in psychology and pop culture as the pillars of a well-lived life. Not the only things, and not necessarily the most important things, but big things—like the legs of a three-legged stool. When one is shaky, the whole thing feels unstable. And you feel it everywhere.

Health: The Body Keeps Score

For years, health was something we didn't have to think much about. Our bodies carried us where we needed to go, absorbed stress, rebounded after late nights, and adapted to whatever we put them through. Until one day, they no longer do. The energy dips. The aches settle in. The doctor mentions cholesterol or blood pressure, and suddenly, health is something we have to tend to.

The mistake we make is thinking that taking care of ourselves requires a complete overhaul. That we need a rigid routine, a disciplined plan, a level of commitment we've never managed before. But real health is built in the spaces between the big commitments. It's the small shifts and daily choices. A short walk instead of skipping movement altogether. Water instead of another coffee. More sleep, less rushing.

Think of your body like a house you've been living in for decades. You can't expect it to stay in perfect shape without maintenance. A little care here, a small repair there—those things add up. Ignore it too long and the foundation starts to crack.

Money: Stress or Freedom?

Money provides security, options, and breathing room. It shapes the choices we make and the ones we believe we have. By midlife, we've had all kinds of experiences with money—earning it, spending it, saving it, and worrying about it. For many, it has been a source of stress more often than a source of freedom. If we're not careful, money stops being a tool and starts feeling like a trap: the endless pursuit of more, the weight of financial decisions, and the quiet fear of not having enough. But money was never meant to be the goal. The goal is to align money with the life we actually want to live.

Think of money like the fuel gauge on your dashboard. You don't need a full tank at all times, but you do need to know how much is there and where it's taking you. The problem isn't the number; it's whether you're on a road that actually leads somewhere you want to go. That doesn't happen through grand financial moves or sudden shifts. It happens in daily decisions: A pause before a purchase. A choice to save rather than spend. A habit that brings clarity rather than avoidance. When money becomes something that supports rather than controls you, everything feels lighter.

Connection: The Quiet Shift

We were made for connection. For people who remind us of who we are, for laughter over dinner, for relationships

You always have two options: Move toward the life you want… or away from it.

———

that hold us up when life feels heavy. But midlife shifts the landscape. Kids grow up. Friendships change. Partnerships stretch in ways we didn't expect. And if we're not intentional, we drift. One day, we look around and realize we feel disconnected—even in a room full of people.

Connection is like a garden. It doesn't flourish on its own. It needs tending, attention, and care. Some relationships thrive with just a little watering, others require pruning, and some will have run their course. This is when we have to decide. Because connection doesn't just happen. It's built, nurtured, and protected. It requires showing up, reaching out, and making the effort even when life feels busy. It means recognizing which relationships bring us life and which ones we've outgrown—not because they were never important, but because they were. Some connections are meant to carry us through a season. Others are meant to evolve with us. Knowing the difference is part of the work of midlife.

The Power of Choice Points

Life shifts don't happen all at once. They happen in small, often unnoticed moments. Every day, we come to choice points, those tiny inflection points that shape our direction, moving us closer to the life we want or pulling us further away from it. The idea of choice points comes from the work of Joseph Ciarrochi, Ann Bailey, and Russ Harris, who describe them as the small, everyday decisions that either align with our values or pull us further from them. Most of the time, these moments are subtle: the decision to go for a short walk instead of scrolling on your phone; the choice to put your energy into a friendship that nourishes you instead of one that drains you; the moment you decide to take action rather than stay stuck in hesitation. No matter where a choice fits on the challenge scale—whether it's a small decision about how to spend the next five minutes or a major life shift—we always have the same two options: move toward the life we want or away from it.

Some choices are easy. Others stretch us. Some feel insignificant in the moment but, repeated over time, create lasting impact. When we ignore them, life starts to feel like a series of reactions rather than something we're actively shaping. But when we recognize these moments for what they are—opportunities to choose our direction—we take back our sense of agency.

Living in the Power of Choice

Every day, we are given another chance. Another choice. Another opportunity to shift the direction of our lives—even if just by a degree or two. If a plane is off course by just one degree, it doesn't look like much in the moment. But over time, that tiny shift takes it somewhere entirely different. And the same is true for us. Life doesn't change in grand, sweeping gestures. It changes in these small, powerful moments. And the best part? We get to choose.

TL;DR

- Health, money, and connection—the Big Three—shape our midlife experience. When one is off, we feel it everywhere.
- Small choices, made consistently, shape the direction of your life far more than big, dramatic moments.
- Choice points are the moments that move us closer to or further from the life we want.
- Life shifts in degrees, not dramatic leaps. Small adjustments now lead to big changes over time.
- Every day, we have the power to choose how we show up and where we're headed.

PAUSE & REFLECT

- Which of the Big Three—health, money, or connection—feels most stable for you right now? Which one needs more attention?
- What small choice could you make today that moves you toward the life you want?
- Where are you reacting instead of intentionally shaping your life?
- Who in your life do you need to reconnect with or let go of?
- What's one habit or belief about health, money, or relationships that might be holding you back?

PART TWO

THE THREE CORE COMMITMENTS

NOW WE'LL ROLL UP our sleeves and tackle the work that truly matters. If Part One was the warm-up, this is the workout—the kind that moves the needle and makes a real impact. But we're not diving in blindly. Three powerful commitments will serve as your blueprint for the journey ahead. These chapters will prepare you for the seven mindset shifts ahead in Part Three. The work you put in here will have a lasting impact.

6

COMMITMENT ONE
LEAD YOUR WHOLE SELF WELL

Balance is not something you find; it's something you create.
JANA KINGSFORD

We are Gathered Here Today

We are gathered here today
not by some great call,
but by that familiar, quiet nudge—
the one that says, "Hey, let's talk,"
where the body, mind, soul, and heart
meet for coffee and a chat.
The body shows up first,
fashionably late, as always,
tired from dragging itself through the day.
It sits down, stretches, and sighs,
"Well, at least we're still upright."
The mind arrives next,

buzzing with ideas and what-ifs,
like a reporter chasing a story.
Finally, it takes a seat, saying,
"We don't need to figure it all out today."
Then comes the soul,
gliding in from some peaceful, timeless place,
humming a tune it's known for ages.
It settles in, serene,
as if it's seen it all before.
The soul says nothing.
Last but not least, the heart makes its entrance,
beating faster than it should,
because it's carrying something heavy.
It takes its place, steadying itself,
and quietly murmurs, "Let's stick together, folks."
And so they sit
in the dim light of early evening,
where nothing needs fixing,
where the day's weight (finally) lifts,
where perfection is just a word in the dictionary,
and they toast to the messiness of life,
finding in each other's company
the simple joy of just being here.

POV: YOU'RE LYING FACE DOWN on a massage table, in one of those rare moments when the world actually feels quiet. The room is dim, the music is soft, and for the first time in what feels like forever, you can actually hear yourself think—or better yet, feel. As the therapist's hands work out the stress you've been carrying, you start to notice something. Your body, your mind, your emotions, your spirit—they're all showing up, whether you've been paying attention to them or not.

It's like those early morning hours before the chaos starts, when you're alone with your coffee and the day hasn't quite taken over yet. In that stillness, you get a glimpse of what's really going on inside. Your body, tired from the grind; your mind, already racing ahead; your emotions, quietly carrying the weight of yesterday; and your spirit, whispering, *Hey, remember me?* And, with each knead, your mind seems to whisper to your body, *All right, I hear you loud and clear*, as if finally acknowledging all the aches and tensions that have been quietly staging a protest. These parts of you are interacting and influencing each other in ways you might not always see. When one part is off, it throws the others out of whack. But when they're all in sync, there's this incredible sense of balance, like you're finally moving through life with a little more ease, a little more grace.

But let's be honest: How often do we really check in with all these parts of ourselves? Most days, we're so busy powering through that we miss the signals that something's out of alignment. We push forward, ignoring the tension, the fatigue, and the little voice inside asking for something more.

This chapter is your invitation to stop, listen, and lead your whole self—body, mind, emotions, and spirit— toward a place of alignment and balance. It's recognizing that true leadership, whether it's in your personal life, your work, or how you show up in the world, starts from within. It starts with understanding and nurturing all the parts of who you are so you can lead with authenticity, courage, and yes, even a little bit of grace.

Leading the Whole You: Self-Leadership Starts Here

Self-leadership begins in the quiet spaces, the daily rhythms, and the little choices no one sees. It is an invitation to wake up, take responsibility, and step in with intention. No grand arrival, no finish line, just the daily practice of showing up and leading yourself well. You are the foundation of your own life—no one else is coming to take that role. It's you, now.

Real growth and real depth show up in moments of alignment, when you start listening to every part of yourself—body, mind, heart, and soul. My friend Lisa Strogal calls this Whole Person intelligence (WPi)—a framework where every part of you (spiritual, mental, emotional, social, and physical) works together in sync. This is more than an inspiring idea; it's a way of life. When we ignore parts of ourselves, life becomes something we just "get through." But when we lead ourselves fully, we stop striving for perfection and start showing up—brave, messy, and true.

You Were There

You've been present for every decision, every leap, and every stumble. Like Andy Stanley says, "I've participated in every bad decision I've ever made." You've also been there for every courageous choice and every time you leaned into curiosity over fear. Self-leadership begins by acknowledging this: You are the one constant in your story. Owning that fact is where real self-leadership starts.

You Can Handle the Truth

You are stronger than you think, capable of facing truths you may be inclined to avoid. Leading yourself begins with honesty—taking stock and being real about where you are. This is not always comfortable, but it creates the foundation for growth. When you can face your own truth without turning away, you make space for meaningful change and self-leadership with the courage to stay curious, to notice what's unfolding, and to engage with it fully, even when the outcome is still taking shape.

Whole-Person Leadership: The Five Dimensions

Most self-leadership models focus on four dimensions: body, mind, heart, and soul. Leading yourself well means stepping into the mess, staying in the tension, and moving through the uncertainty with open eyes. It is how you handle the curveballs, how you stay grounded when everything feels shaky, and how you choose to be present when checking out would be easier. It is not about getting it perfect. It is showing up, over and over, with courage and curiosity. Leadership starts on the inside. That's why WPi recognizes a critical fifth element: our meaningful connections.

Self-leadership is stepping into the tension between what is and what could be. It is finding your footing when everything feels unsteady. It is paying attention to who you are and making sure that lines up with how you move through the world. Too often, self-leadership is treated like a solo sport—something you master on your own. But real self-leadership—the kind that lasts, expands, and matters—happens in relationship, in movement, and in the places where life is actually being lived.

You are not just a body moving through habits, a mind full of thoughts, a heart carrying emotions, or a soul searching for meaning. You are all of these things, woven together, pulsing, shifting, growing, and becoming. Leadership is moving forward with intention, with curiosity, and with a deep awareness of the forces shaping you. Self-leadership is showing up. It's making the next right choice, then the next. It's holding the tensions between ambition and rest, confidence and curiosity, and structure and flexibility, knowing that wisdom lives in the space between opposites.

Body: The foundation. Energy, resilience, and physical well-being influence how we lead ourselves. Self-leadership starts with listening—tuning in to the signals of fatigue, movement, and nourishment. A well-led body sustains the rhythm you need, allowing you to move through life with strength and endurance.

Mind: The driver of clarity and innovation. A well-led mind is open, engaged, and adaptable. Growth doesn't happen in comfort. It happens when we learn, stretch, and ask better questions. When we challenge our thinking,

Self-leadership begins in the quiet spaces, the daily rhythms, **and the little choices no one sees.**

---

we make better decisions and sharpen our ability to lead ourselves effectively.

Heart: The center of trust and emotional agility. Your heart isn't a weakness; it tells you what matters. Emotional intelligence helps you stay connected to yourself and others, allowing you to lead with empathy and strength. Self-leadership is learning to work with your emotions, not against them. It is paying attention to what rises up and letting it teach you and move through you without taking over. It is staying steady, staying connected, and showing up fully—right here, right now.

Soul: The compass that points toward meaning. Leading from the soul means knowing what you stand for and ensuring your choices align with those values. A well-led soul doesn't need external validation; it is centered in purpose, giving you the clarity to move with conviction.

Connection: The often-overlooked but essential dimension of self-leadership. No one leads themselves in isolation. The relationships you cultivate shape your perspective, influence your decisions, and provide the support needed to sustain growth. Connection happens when we listen deeply, show up for each other, and allow others to show up for us too.

So here we are. Self-leadership is staying in the questions, paying attention to what pulls you forward, and moving in step with what matters. It is learning to lead yourself well in body, mind, heart, and soul and to connect so you can show up fully right where you are. Because when these five elements are in rhythm, leadership isn't something you do; it's something you embody every day, in every interaction and in every choice.

Balance and Self-Leadership

At one point, I thought I might write a whole book on this: the art of balance and self-leadership, the *it* factor—the ability to hold two seemingly opposing forces in tension without losing your center. I've seen it in great leaders, in wise mentors, and in the kind of people who make life seem effortless, even when you know it isn't. The ones who somehow manage to be fiercely driven and deeply at peace. Future-focused and fully present. Courageous and careful.

Midlife is where this balancing act takes on a new urgency. It's a season where the external markers of success lose their grip and we're left asking, "What now?" This is when self-leadership moves from chasing to listening. It stops being a race for more and becomes a rhythm that fits. It is less about what the world demands and more about what feels true, deep down, where it matters. I know people who have built entire careers on hustle and external validation, only to hit midlife and realize they don't recognize themselves anymore. Self-leadership in midlife means redefining success and allowing space for reinvention.

I think about my friend who built a thriving business while raising three kids, navigating uncertainty with this quiet steadiness, never rushing but never stagnant. She once told me, "You have to learn to trust the rhythm of things. When to push, when to pull back. When to speak up, when to just listen." That stuck with me. Because that's the work of self-leadership. It's knowing when to take control and when to let go, when to move forward and when to pause, when to lean in and when to step back. It's navigating the tension between confidence and humility—knowing your strengths but staying open to growth. It's understanding that speed isn't always the answer, but neither is hesitation. That introspection matters, but so does being attuned to the people around you.

There was a moment in my own life when I realized I was trying to force a chapter that had already ended. I had spent years identifying with a particular role, pushing through because that's what I thought leaders did—keep going, no matter what. But then life sent a series of small signals: exhaustion that wouldn't lift, a sense of disengagement in work that once brought joy, a quiet voice inside whispering, *What if you let go?* Self-leadership, in that moment, wasn't about powering through. It was about pausing, reassessing, and having the courage to step into something new.

The balancing act never ends. It shifts with seasons, roles, and what life throws at us. But the ones who lead themselves well don't just survive that tension; they learn to thrive within it.

Consistency: The Backbone of Self-Leadership

Consistency builds self-trust. It's the quiet work; the unflashy, unsexy, everyday stuff. Making your bed. Closing your laptop when you said you would. Showing up for ten minutes of reflection when you'd rather scroll through real estate listings. It's the kind of practice that rarely gets applause but somehow keeps you grounded.

I remember picking up the book *Celebration of Discipline* by Richard Foster when I was younger, and my first thought was, "This might not be my book." Celebration? Of discipline? Those words seemed disconnected in my world.

Some parts of my life lend themselves to discipline. Work comes naturally. I can meet deadlines, stay focused, and follow through. But in other areas—exercise, rest, setting limits—it gets murky. Some people seem wired for structure. I've had to inch my way toward it, usually while trying to convince myself that walking the dog counts as cardio.

But naming the struggle was a turning point, not because I had conquered it, but because I stopped pretending I should have. That's where consistency begins to do its work. Not in perfection, but in practice. Not in impressing anyone, but in becoming someone you can count on. Even when you're still figuring it out.

When Life Feels Out of Sync

Sometimes, everything feels off. You wake up tired. You're short with the people you love. You skip the workout, forget the meeting, and stare at your screen like it owes you something. You eat junk, scroll too much, and feel weirdly emotional about a commercial for paper towels. It's like your body, mind, heart, and soul are all playing different songs at the same time.

The first step is noticing. Not fixing, just naming it. That's how you start to come back. Self-leadership means checking in with all of you. When one part is off, the rest feel it, but when they begin to move together again, even a little, you start to find your rhythm. That's when you lead with clarity and steadiness.

Reflection and Renewal: A Lifelong Journey

Self-leadership is an ongoing process. It requires checking in, reflecting, and adjusting as life unfolds. It's about leading a life that feels true to who you are becoming. At its heart is self-awareness. Whole Person intelligence helps us align every part of ourselves—body, mind, heart, soul, and social self—to create a life that is rich, resilient, and real. And that's the kind of life that matters, both for us and for those we impact along the way.

TL;DR

- Self-leadership is about alignment, not control. It's the ability to tune in, adapt, and lead yourself with clarity and purpose.

- True leadership starts within. You can't lead others effectively if you're not leading yourself with awareness and intention.

- Your whole self—body, mind, heart, soul, and connections—works together. Ignoring one part throws everything off balance.

- Balance isn't something you find; it's something you create. Knowing when to push, when to pause, and when to recalibrate is key.

- Midlife is a powerful reset. It's a shift from chasing success to living in alignment with what truly matters.

- Great self-leaders embrace the tension. They hold ambition and rest, confidence and humility, structure and fluidity—thriving in the space between.

PAUSE & REFLECT

- Where are you leading yourself in a way that feels true, aligned, and grounded? And then, where could you lean in a little more, dig a little deeper, and get a little more honest?

- What area of your life has been nudging you for attention, and how can you start showing up for it?

- How often do you pause to listen to what your body, heart, and mind are telling you? What might you hear if you did?

7

COMMITMENT TWO
TELL YOURSELF THE TRUTH

Honesty is the first chapter in the book of wisdom.
THOMAS JEFFERSON

Unburdened

It starts in
that quiet, in-between space
where the noise fades
and it's just you.
No excuses,
no distractions,
just a raw, unfiltered
you.
And in that moment,
the truth shows up.
Not to scold,
not to shame,

but to ask:
"Are you ready yet?"
The truth doesn't shout.
It doesn't force its way in.
It just waits—
patient, steady, unyielding—
until you're tired of pretending.
Because you know.
You've always known.
It's that little tug in your chest,
that whisper in the back of your mind,
the thing you've been avoiding.
The truth isn't cruel,
but it can be sharp.
It'll slice through your excuses,
peel back your justifications,
and leave you standing there,
vulnerable
but free.
The truth doesn't show up to punish you.
It's here to liberate you.
To remind you that
you don't have to carry untruth anymore.
And when truth surfaces,
you'll breathe again.
You'll stand taller.
And you'll move forward,
Unburdened.

POV: IT'S THE END of a long, draining day, and you're standing in front of the mirror. You expect to see the usual tired face staring back at you, but tonight, something feels different. As you look closer, you're not just seeing your physical reflection; you're seeing the entire scope of your life. The choices you've made, the paths you've walked, and the truths you've been avoiding start to surface. That small, persistent voice within—the one you've been trying to drown out with busyness, distractions, and little white lies—begins to grow louder. It's the voice that whispers about the career that feels more like a cage than a calling, or the relationship that's become more routine than true connection. As you try to muster a smile, it feels forced, like a mask that's become all too familiar but no longer fits.

This moment in front of the mirror is significant. It's not just a glance at your reflection; it's a moment of reckoning. It exposes the comfort we find in our self-deceptions—the stories we spin about "just getting by" or "waiting for the right time." But as you stand there, you realize these comforting fictions are starting to crumble. The façade you've built is beginning to show its cracks, and what's left is the unvarnished truth you've been avoiding.

Self-honesty means tearing down the walls of pretense and confronting the raw reality of who you are. It's the act of looking at yourself, your life, and your choices without the rose-colored glasses, and it's not easy. This chapter is a call to face those truths head-on, because truth, while uncomfortable and sometimes daunting, is the key to unlocking a life that feels more real, more fulfilling, and truly your own.

Embracing self-honesty can feel like swimming against the current. We live in a society that bombards us with noise—social media, endless to-do lists, and the constant pressure to conform to what's expected. It's all too easy to get swept up in this whirlwind and lose touch with the quiet voice inside—the one that speaks uncomfortable truths we'd rather ignore. But imagine finding a moment of stillness, a pause in the midst of all this chaos, where you can truly listen to that voice. This is where self-honesty begins: in those quiet moments when you strip away the external noise and connect with the core of who you are. It's recognizing and accepting the reality of your life without the filters of external validation or societal expectations. It involves peeling back the layers of what the world tells you to be and confronting the reality of your own dreams, fears, and choices.

Self-honesty is an act of courage. It means being willing to face truths that might challenge the image you've constructed of yourself or that push you out of your comfort zone. It's acknowledging where you've been avoiding the hard conversations with yourself and, instead, choosing to engage with them fully. It's not being harsh or critical; it's being real, being kind to yourself, and understanding that true growth comes from a place of deep, honest self-reflection.

In this chapter, we'll delve into how self-honesty can act as a catalyst for real, meaningful change. We'll explore the stories of individuals who have dared to confront their own truths—people who have looked themselves in the eye and asked the hard questions and, in doing so, transformed their lives. These are stories of personal growth and of discovering that by aligning more closely with who we truly are, we unlock the potential for deeper connections with others and a more profound impact on the world around us.

The truth, while sometimes painful, is liberating. When we stop hiding from ourselves, we open the door to a life that is more authentic, more grounded, and ultimately more fulfilling. And it all begins with that moment of honesty: looking in the mirror and choosing to see, really see, who we are.

The Moment You Stop Lying to Yourself

There comes a point when the story we've been telling ourselves stops making sense—when the justifications feel thin, the excuses fall apart, and the truth, no matter how uncomfortable, is the only thing left. These moments don't come with fanfare. They don't happen in dramatic montages set to inspirational music. They happen in quiet, ordinary spaces—on a hiking trail, in an office meeting, or in the kitchen at the end of a long day.

In my work as a coach, I've had the privilege of walking alongside people as they wrestled with their own truths. I've watched high-performing executives admit that the careers they built no longer fit. I've seen parents come to terms with the fact that they've been absent in

The truth doesn't arrive to punish you. **It's here to unburden you.**

---

ways that matter. I've worked with people confronting long-avoided conversations about money, relationships, addiction, and identity. The hardest thing isn't the truth itself; it's letting go of the illusion that things are fine when they're not.

Mateo had been successful in his job for years, moving up, taking on bigger roles, and building a reputation as someone who got things done. But lately, work felt harder, not because he wasn't capable but because it didn't energize him anymore. He was spending more time managing than actually doing the work he loved, sitting through meetings where he had less and less to contribute. He kept telling himself to push through, that it was just a rough patch. But one day, in the middle of yet another meeting, he caught himself zoning out, barely following the discussion. And he thought, "I don't want to be here." That night, instead of brushing it off, he let himself sit with it. And he started asking the real question: "If this isn't it anymore, then what is?"

Olivia never considered herself a heavy drinker. It was just a glass of wine after work. Then another while making dinner. One more before bed. She wasn't reckless; just unwinding. But one morning, she went to pour herself coffee and realized she couldn't remember the last night she hadn't had a drink. That thought sat heavy in her chest. She tried skipping the wine that evening, just to see if she could. It was harder than she expected. That was her answer.

Victor had a good job, a comfortable life, and an ironclad habit of avoiding his bank account. He made good money, but he spent more. He told himself he'd deal with it later. Then, one day, his card was declined at a coffee shop. He laughed it off, but later that night he finally opened his banking app. He stared at the numbers, exhaled, and let the truth sink in.

Luca had always believed he was deeply involved in his son's life. He coached his soccer team, attended every game, and talked strategy on the drive home. But lately, his son seemed different. Less engaged, less excited. He still played well, but the fire was gone. One evening, Luca caught a glimpse of scars on his son's arm. He didn't say anything at first, but that night, sitting alone in the kitchen, the weight of it settled in: "I know his stats and his tournament schedule, but I don't know what's really going on with him." Soccer had been their shared language, but now it felt like a shield, a way to avoid harder conversations. And suddenly, Luca realized something had to shift. Their relationship couldn't just be about the game. It had to be about him.

These moments of reckoning don't come with applause. No one celebrates when you finally stop running. But they are sacred. They are the threshold between who you've been and who you're about to become. And if you can stay with that discomfort—if you can hold your own gaze just a little longer than feels comfortable—you might just find that honesty isn't an ending at all. It's the beginning of something real.

The Hidden Costs of Ignoring Self-Honesty

Imagine your life as a house with a leaky roof. Instead of fixing it, you keep covering the cracks, slapping on patches, and painting over the stains. It might seem fine for a while, but eventually, the damage worsens—mold, rot, and real structural problems. This is what happens when we gloss over uncomfortable truths instead of facing them head-on. We pay a steep price, and the cost affects us in real, concrete ways.

Eroding self-trust: Think of self-trust as a bridge between your inner self and the world. Every time you deny the truth, a piece of that bridge weakens. Little by little, the bridge becomes shaky, and you start doubting your own judgment. This disconnection from your true self seeps into everything, making it harder to trust not just yourself but others too. Ignoring truth doesn't keep us safe; it chips away at the core of who we are.

Stunted growth: Choosing comfort over truth also stunts our growth. It's like trimming the tops of weeds while ignoring the roots. Sure, it looks tidy for a while, but those weeds keep coming back. Self-deception keeps us in these same cycles, playing small and sticking to safe patterns. Without digging deep, we miss out on who we could be and what we're truly capable of.

Strained relationships: Our relationships don't escape this fallout, either. When we're not honest with ourselves, we're building a house on shifting sands. Trying to connect with others while presenting an inauthentic version of ourselves only creates a shaky foundation. Over time, misunderstandings creep in, and what could be a genuine connection becomes shallow and strained. True relationships require a foundation of honesty, and that starts with showing up as who we really are.

The emotional toll: Picture carrying around a backpack filled with stones, each one a truth you've been avoiding. Every time you dodge reality, another stone gets added. Eventually, the weight becomes exhausting. The effort it takes to maintain a façade drains our energy, leading to stress, dissatisfaction, and a sense of disconnection from our true emotions. Avoiding truth weighs us down.

Impaired decision-making and compromised integrity: Self-deception clouds our judgment. It's like trying to steer a ship in fog without a compass. When we aren't honest with ourselves, we're navigating life without direction, basing decisions on half-truths and distortions. Making choices that align with our values when we're not seeing things as they really are is tough. When we avoid self-honesty, we compromise our personal integrity. Living authentically means aligning our beliefs, values, and actions in a way that feels true. Shying away from truth disrupts that alignment, eroding our self-worth and fulfillment.

How to Get Real with Yourself

Create space for reflection: Start by giving yourself space to reflect. Find a spot where you can be alone with your thoughts—a cozy corner, a peaceful spot in nature, or even a favorite café. Use this time to sit with your feelings and ask yourself the questions you've been avoiding. Writing in a journal can help untangle emotions and bring clarity to what you're experiencing. This is your time to be honest with yourself, without judgment.

Tune into your inner voice: Mindfulness is one of the best tools we have for connecting with our true selves. Engage in practices like meditation, deep breathing, or even walking in nature. These practices help us listen to the subtle truths within—the quiet, often drowned-out voice that speaks when we're still. The more you tune in, the easier it becomes to see through comforting stories and identify the truths that truly matter.

Challenge your avoidance: We all have ways of sidestepping the truths we'd rather not face—through distractions, rationalizations, or keeping up appearances. Start by noticing your own avoidance tactics. Ask yourself, "What am I really afraid of?" By understanding the fears that keep us from facing truth, we can confront them with more courage and resolve. This step is crucial in building an honest relationship with yourself.

Seek honest feedback: Sometimes, we need help to see what we can't see in ourselves. Reach out to trusted friends, family, or mentors for a perspective you might be missing. Their feedback can reveal patterns you've been blind to. Be open to their insights, even when they challenge your beliefs. Their honesty is a gift that can guide you toward greater self-awareness and growth.

Start small, dream big: Self-honesty doesn't have to be overwhelming. Begin with small, manageable steps that lead you closer to the truth. If you're considering a big change, like a career shift, start with something simple, like researching new opportunities or updating your resume. Small actions build confidence and make confronting deeper truths more approachable. Over time, these small steps accumulate, leading to big, transformative changes.

Embrace the process: Self-honesty is a continuous journey. It's not about reaching a perfect state of truth but about embracing the ongoing process of discovery. Be kind to yourself as you walk this path. Every step toward facing the truth brings you closer to a life that feels real and grounded. Progress, not perfection.

The Power of Embracing Our Truths

When we face the truth, even the painful parts, it's like stepping into light after a long, dark night. Truth cuts through the fog, letting us see ourselves with fresh clarity. When we confront reality, we strip away the illusions holding us back, opening the door to living more authentically and discovering who we really are beneath all the layers. This creates space for genuine self-acceptance. Knowing who we are, strengths and imperfections alike, lets us stand confidently in the world. This is the work of recognizing and embracing our worth, exactly as we are. When we accept our truth, we gain resilience, navigating life with a peace that only comes from knowing ourselves deeply.

Additionally, when we're truthful with ourselves, we naturally bring more authenticity into our connections. Relationships thrive on honesty, and this kind of honesty fosters trust and strengthens bonds with the people who matter most. By showing up as our true selves, we invite others to do the same, creating genuine and lasting relationships.

Truth-telling is that powerful. It may be uncomfortable, but it sets the stage for meaningful change. When we stop denying or avoiding what's real, we open ourselves to new possibilities and the chance to evolve. Facing truth unlocks potential and leads us down a path of personal growth. And no matter how difficult, it brings us closer to a life that's truly aligned with who we are. It's a journey toward fulfillment, where we live in harmony with our values and desires. Facing uncomfortable truths clears the path to a richer, deeper, more authentic life.

The Science Behind Self-Honesty

Picture a crossroads: One path leads to comfort and familiar routines; the other veers into the unknown, demanding we confront hidden truths. This is where self-honesty meets us—challenging, uncomfortable, but ultimately transformative.

Many of us, understandably, choose the path of least resistance. We tell ourselves small deceits: "I'm fine"; "Things will get better on their own"; "I can handle this later." Psychologists call this self-deception—a defense that shields us from painful truths. It's like wearing sunglasses indoors: The light feels less harsh, but your perception becomes distorted. Yet, the same research showing the dangers of self-deception also reveals the way out. Embracing self-honesty is one of the most effective paths to growth and mental health. Honest self-reflection opens doors to self-awareness, clarity about values, and a life aligned with who we really are.

Self-honesty is like a mirror that doesn't just show our reflection but reveals the state of our inner world. This clarity might bring discomfort, but it's also a motivator for change. By acknowledging our inner truths, we can align our actions with our beliefs, leading to a more integrated, fulfilling life.

Choosing the Harder Path

The journey to self-honesty isn't easy, but it's worth it. Choosing the harder path, the one that asks us to be real, ultimately leads to an authentic, satisfying life. As we navigate this journey, our decision-making improves, our relationships deepen, and our sense of self becomes stronger and more grounded.

If you're curious about the science behind self-honesty (how self-deception works, why cognitive dissonance matters, and the many benefits of self-awareness) explore more on the *Shift* website. There, I break down the research and offer tools to help you on your path toward a more honest, authentic life.

TL;DR

- Facing the truth, even when uncomfortable, is crucial for authentic self-discovery and growth.
- Being honest with yourself fosters self-acceptance and inner peace.
- Acknowledging the truth is a catalyst for change—it leads to personal transformation and opens doors to new opportunities.
- Honesty strengthens and enhances relationships by building trust and genuine connections.
- While challenging, embracing the truth leads to a more fulfilling and joyful life.
- Self-deception is comfortable, but by challenging it you realize that the stories you've told yourself to get by are starting to crumble.
- Self-honesty is about tearing down the pretense and facing the raw truth of who you are, even when it's uncomfortable.

- Self-honesty is powerful. Embracing the truth leads to personal growth, deeper connections, and a more fulfilling life.

PAUSE & REFLECT

- What truths about yourself have you been avoiding, and how might facing them change your life?
- How do your current beliefs and self-deceptions impact your growth?
- In what ways have you used excuses or masks to avoid uncomfortable truths, and what are they protecting you from?
- How can embracing self-honesty improve your relationships with others?
- What steps can you take to create a more honest and authentic relationship with yourself?

8

COMMITMENT THREE
PRACTICE RADICAL ACCEPTANCE

Acceptance doesn't mean resignation. It means understanding and dealing straightforwardly.
MICHAEL J. FOX

Where I Stand

The time has come
when the winds howl
and the storm shakes the earth,
and I stand, not resisting—
but letting it pass through me,
feeling its weight,
saying, "This is where I am."
In the mirror of my life,

my life lines weave stories,
each a truth, a testament to who I am.
No more hiding,
no turning away—
I honor dreams that have taken root,
fears that have faded,
and I say, "This is who I am."
Acceptance, not surrender;
quiet strength to hold what is,
to cradle pain and joy,
not to change, not to fix,
but to let them be,
let them breathe.
There's freedom here—
respite from what could be.
In stillness, I find power,
knowing I am whole,
worthy, as I am.
I walk with strength,
not because life is easy,
but because I am true—
a blend of light and shadow,
sorrow and joy.
This is my truth, I say;
I will live it fully.

I REMEMBER SITTING in a circle with Rob Bell, an author, speaker, and artist whose thought-provoking questions and profound observations never fail to stir the soul. We were in Ojai, California, where twenty curious minds had gathered to explore some of life's big questions. What an experience that was—spending time under the shade of towering palms, surrounded by ancient oaks and olive trees, with the fragrant scent of citrus and sage in the air and the distant hum of cicadas.

It was in this tranquil setting that Rob introduced the concept of "owning every square inch of your story." This idea was a gentle yet profound nudge. It was like he handed me a mirror, allowing me to see my whole story— the beautiful, the painful, the messy, and the triumphant. It wasn't a revelation but a reinforcement of something I had always known, yet it took on new meaning that day. It moved me from being a passive participant in my life to an active creator of my future. I realized that every part of my journey, every scar and every success, was integral to who I am.

Life can be a lot like a hot air balloon. In the beginning, we put everything we have into filling it with air. We work hard. We build. We push. We are determined to get ourselves off the ground. What we do not realize is that along the way we pick up sandbags. Some are expectations we never agreed to, some are ambitions that once mattered but do not anymore, and some are fears disguised as goals. By the time we reach midlife, the balloon is heavy. It's full, but it's not lifting the way we imagined. We start to question why—why the striving that once propelled us forward now feels like it's holding us down. And then, gently, we begin to see: Rising isn't about adding more air; it's about releasing the weight.

It's not about doing more but about carrying less. The shift we long for comes through permission, not force—permission to feel what we've been holding, to name what no longer fits, and to begin the work of letting go. That's when lift happens. Not in the push, but in the release.

Moments of Realization

A coaching client once shared a moment that changed everything. Alone in her kitchen, stirring a pot of soup, she felt the weight of something she had carried for most of her adult life—a deep regret she had spent years outrunning. It wasn't a sudden revelation but a quiet reckoning. She had built a life around avoiding it, convincing herself it didn't matter. But in that stillness, something cracked open. She set down the spoon, leaned against the counter, and let it in. Maybe she didn't have to keep fighting it. There were no instant answers, no neat resolutions. But in that moment, she made a choice to stop resisting and start allowing. And that choice, small as it seemed, was the beginning of real change.

Another client had been carrying a weight for years—so long he had stopped questioning it. He pictured himself dragging a heavy suitcase, one so familiar it just felt like part of him. Never thought to open it or stopped to look inside. But one day, he did. And there it was: guilt. Heavy, familiar, worn from being carried so long. And underneath it? Shame. The kind that settles in deep, convincing you that you are the sum of your worst moments.

What if peace isn't found in fixing the past but in **learning to hold it with kindness?**

———————

He had kept lugging it forward, believing he had to and that setting it down would mean ignoring it, excusing it.

And then came the question: "Do I actually have to keep carrying this?" The answer didn't come all at once. Letting go never works like that. But little by little, he started unpacking. Holding his guilt up to the light. Asking if shame was telling him the truth—or just a story he had come to believe. What he discovered didn't require forcing himself to move on or pretending the past didn't happen. It was something else entirely: a way of seeing things as they really were, loosening his grip, and finally making space for something new

Enter Radical Acceptance

Radical acceptance is the courageous and transformative practice of embracing reality exactly as it is—no embellishments, no denial, just the unvarnished truth. This isn't about giving up or waving a white flag at life's challenges. Instead, it's making a deliberate choice to meet life head-on, with an open heart and a clear mind. Radical acceptance allows us to stop resisting what is and to start engaging with our lives more fully, with all their messiness, complexity, and beauty.

Embracing Reality

Life is unpredictable. It doesn't always adhere to our carefully laid plans or meet our expectations. Radical acceptance asks us to recognize and embrace this unpredictability and see our circumstances for what they truly are, without trying to mold them into something else. This practice doesn't mean abandoning our dreams or hopes; rather, it's beginning from a place of truth. By accepting where we are, we can move forward with a sense of clarity and purpose, grounded in reality rather than in illusion.

Letting Go of Control

There's a deep freedom that comes with letting go of the need to control every aspect of our lives. We often believe that if we just try hard enough, we can force the world to bend to our will. But radical acceptance teaches us that real power lies in recognizing what we cannot change. It requires us to focus on what we can control and release the rest. This is an active decision to find peace amid life's uncertainties and to trust that we can navigate whatever comes our way with grace and resilience.

Cultivating Compassion

Radical acceptance also means cultivating deep compassion—for ourselves and for others. It's acknowledging that being human means being imperfect and that suffering and joy are intertwined parts of our experience. This compassion helps us to stop fighting against ourselves and let go of the harsh judgments that often keep us stuck. When we approach life with compassion, we allow ourselves to grow from our experiences and see our flaws not as failures but as integral parts of our journey.

The Origins of Radical Acceptance

Radical acceptance, as we know it today, owes much to the insights and experiences of Dr. Marsha Linehan, the pioneering psychologist who developed dialectical behavior therapy (DBT). Her approach to mental health treatment, particularly for those struggling with intense emotional pain, is deeply rooted in the concept of radical acceptance.

Linehan's own life story is a testament to the power of radical acceptance. As a young woman, she battled severe mental illness, spending years in psychiatric hospitals where she was often labeled as beyond help. During one of her lowest moments, confined to a seclusion room, she had an epiphany. She realized that fighting against her reality only deepened her suffering. Instead, she made the choice to accept herself as she was, without judgment. This was the beginning of a profound transformation. Through this acceptance, Linehan found the strength to move forward and ultimately developed DBT, a therapy that has since saved countless lives.

Radical acceptance is powerful, but to grasp its true essence, it's important to understand what it is not:

It's not resignation: Acceptance isn't about giving up. It's seeing things clearly so we can move forward with wisdom and purpose.

It's not endorsing harm: Accepting reality doesn't mean condoning injustice or staying in harmful situations. It means seeing things as they are so we can take meaningful action.

It's not avoiding emotions: True acceptance allows us to feel everything—the joy, pain, and uncertainty—without being controlled by those emotions.

Moving Toward Radical Acceptance

Acceptance allows us to shift from resistance to resilience and from avoidance to engagement. It empowers us to face reality, make intentional choices, and move forward with clarity. Here's how it works:

Healing emotional pain: When we stop resisting our emotions and allow ourselves to feel them, we create space for healing.

Reducing suffering: Much of our suffering comes from wishing things were different. Acceptance relieves us of that burden.

Empowering action: When we accept what is, we can focus on what we can change.

Fostering resilience: Facing reality builds inner strength and equips us to handle challenges with more grace.

Enhancing relationships: Accepting others as they are fosters deeper, more genuine connections.

So, how do we practice radical acceptance? It starts with small steps:

1. **Acknowledge what is:** Name the situation, feeling, or experience you've been resisting.
2. **Allow emotions to surface:** Let yourself feel what you feel without judgment.
3. **Identify what you can and cannot control:** Shift your focus to what's within your power.
4. **Practice mindfulness:** Stay present instead of getting lost in regrets or worries.
5. **Cultivate self-compassion:** Speak to yourself with kindness, as you would to a friend.

Radical Acceptance and Trauma

Radical acceptance may sound straightforward, but it is not easy. And when it comes to healing from trauma, it's often best to work with a therapist. Some people have faced experiences they should never have had to endure, and no simple mindset shift can dissolve that pain overnight. Trauma leaves deep imprints—on our bodies, our emotions, and the way we see the world. Radical acceptance does not mean dismissing what happened or minimizing the impact. Instead, it invites us to hold space for our pain while finding ways to move forward, at our own pace, with support and care.

Healing is a process—one that unfolds over time, with patience and care. If radical acceptance is the bridge, self-compassion is the steady ground beneath our feet, reminding us that we are worthy of healing and that we don't have to walk this road alone.

TL;DR

- Embrace your whole story. Every experience—good, bad, messy—shapes who you are. Acceptance is owning it all, not just the easy parts.

- Fighting reality drains energy. Letting go of what you can't change frees you to focus on what you can.

- Acceptance is not giving up. It's facing life honestly so you can respond with clarity and strength.

- Control is an illusion. The need to control everything fuels stress. Acceptance helps shift focus to what's actually within your power.

- Discomfort is the price of growth. Avoidance, denial, and perfectionism may feel safer, but they keep you stuck. Acceptance clears the way forward.

- Radical acceptance is a skill—it takes practice. Acknowledge feelings, challenge resistance, and meet life with openness and self-compassion.

PAUSE & REFLECT

- What parts of your life have you been resisting, and how might embracing them bring peace?

- How can you begin to "own every square inch" of your story, including the messy parts?

- In what ways have you been trying to control outcomes, and what would letting go look like for you?

- How might practicing radical acceptance change the way you approach challenges in your life?

PART THREE

SEVEN MINDSET SHIFTS FOR AN INSPIRED MIDLIFE

WELCOME TO PART THREE, where we explore the seven mindset shifts that can redefine how you experience the second half of life. This is about making meaningful changes that fill life with purpose, joy, and connection. These mindset shifts are more than ideas; they're practical strategies grounded in research, designed to help you think differently and live more fully. Each shift invites you into a deeper, more intentional way of living so you can move through the world with greater clarity and purpose. Let's step in together and see where they lead.

9
SHIFT INTO CURIOSITY
RELEASE THE SHACKLES OF CERTAINTY

Embrace uncertainty. Some of the most beautiful chapters in our lives won't have a title until much later.
BOB GOFF

The Shackles of Certainty

We hang on to what we know
like it's the last cookie at the bottom of the jar.
Clutching the familiar,
wrapped up in routine like a warm, scratchy blanket
we've convinced ourselves is cashmere.
But the real trouble isn't what we don't know;
it's all the stuff we think we do.
The tidy little boxes we tick,
the answers we parrot,

the stories we tell ourselves
at bedtime to keep the monsters away.
Meanwhile, life's out there,
wild and unbothered,
waving its arms and yelling,
"Come have a look at *this*!"
There's a sky with no signs,
a road with no railing,
and curiosity dancing in its underpants,
waiting for someone to join in.
When we finally let go—
of being right,
of being certain,
of knowing everything all the time—
we breathe.
And in that breath,
we find something better than safety.
We find life.
Messy, surprising, beautifully uncertain life.

FOR MUCH OF MY LIFE, I thought certainty was the goal. Knowing the right answers, making the right choices, having a plan—that felt like success. Certainty was a warm, well-lit room, a place where I could feel safe, assured, and in control.

But life has a way of challenging our certainties, sometimes in quiet moments of doubt, other times in sudden, jarring upheavals. A career shift that forces us to question our identity. A relationship that doesn't unfold the way we expected. A deeply held belief that, over time, starts to feel like a sweater that doesn't quite fit anymore.

I've come to see that certainty, while comforting, can also become a set of invisible shackles. It can keep us in places we've outgrown, limit our ability to adapt, and prevent us from stepping into something new. The older I get, the more I believe that curiosity—not certainty—is what keeps life expansive, meaningful, and alive.

Looking back, I can see the moments when certainty kept me stuck. The times I made choices based on what I thought I should do rather than what truly called to me. The times I ignored the small, nagging feeling that something wasn't right because I didn't want to disrupt the structure I had built.

But here's what I've learned: Certainty is an illusion. Life is unpredictable, people change, and even the beliefs we once held tightly can shift with experience and wisdom. The real question isn't whether we can hold onto certainty, but whether we can loosen our grip on it enough to let curiosity lead us into something new.

Faith and Certainty

For those who, like me, were raised with a faith, our relationship with certainty is often layered and nuanced. Faith can act like a trusted map, guiding us along the well-trodden paths that have been walked by countless souls before us. There's a promise in that map—a comforting assurance that if we "stay the course," everything will unfold according to a divine plan. This map doesn't just offer comfort; it instills a deep sense of direction and purpose, anchoring us in the midst of an unpredictable world.

Yet faith invites us into this dance between certainty and mystery. What if the divine—that mystery we call God—is so vast, so endlessly profound, that it blows apart every boundary we try to place around it? Like Hamlet said to Horatio, "There are more things in Heaven and Earth than are dreamt of in your philosophy." Embracing uncertainty doesn't lessen our faith; it stretches it. It calls us to release the need to understand everything in tidy terms, to let go of our labels and definitions, and step into something far greater.

This is the kind of faith that expands and opens, the kind that whispers, "There's more"—more wonder, more depth, and more meaning woven into every corner of existence. It's a faith that doesn't just answer but asks, that draws us deeper into the vastness of a reality we can only begin to glimpse. And maybe that's the point. Because the divine isn't meant to be contained; it's meant to stir our hearts, to call us to awe, to keep us wondering.

For those who find comfort and guidance in these maps, it's important to honor that. These maps are invaluable; they help us navigate life's complexities with peace and confidence. In fact, research consistently shows a positive correlation between faith and numerous aspects of well-being. But there may come a time when even the most familiar paths lead us to unexpected detours and to challenges that stretch our understanding, even with faith. In these moments, the journey deepens. Faith calls us to open ourselves to a broader, richer experience with the divine. We can embrace the wonder, the awe, and the mystery that make our spiritual journey so meaningful. At its heart, faith isn't having all the answers; it's living with trust, embracing the unknown, and believing that the journey itself will lead us to the insights and growth we need.

As we release the need for certainty, we open ourselves up to the possibility that there's more beauty, more wonder, and more truth than we could ever imagine. We celebrate the mystery, the uncontainable, and the wildness of it all and trust that in doing so, we can find a deeper, more authentic connection to the divine and to ourselves. Because in the end, it's in the letting go, in the embrace of mystery, that real transformation begins.

Beyond Certainty: The Courage to Embrace the Unknown

In our quest for stability and control, we often cling to certainty as if it were a lifeline. It feels safe, providing order in an unpredictable world. But certainty can also become a cage, limiting our growth and keeping us from exploring our full potential. When we are too convinced that we know how things should be, we close ourselves off to new possibilities.

Certainty, in its most rigid form, prevents us from embracing fresh perspectives and adapting to change.

Certainty may keep us comfortable, **but curiosity keeps us alive.**

It anchors us to a fixed mindset—where the world is seen in black and white, right and wrong, known and unknown. This mindset may be comforting, but it stifles creativity, limits experiences, and keeps us from fully living. The more we cling to certainty, the more we resist the very changes that could lead to growth and fulfillment. Richard Rohr's words, "We do not think ourselves into new ways of living, we live ourselves into new ways of thinking," challenge our attachment to certainty. They invite us to step into the unknown—the messy, unpredictable process of living. True mindset shifts don't come from intellectual understanding alone but from experience, from letting life shape us.

The Power of Curiosity

If certainty is a cage, then curiosity is the key that unlocks it. Curiosity allows us to approach life with wonder and see each moment as an opportunity to learn and grow. It shifts our focus from needing to be right to being open, and from protecting our beliefs to exploring new ideas. Curiosity keeps us flexible and adaptable—essential qualities for real transformation. When we embrace curiosity, we release the need to have all the answers. We understand that not knowing is not a failure but an invitation. It shifts us from stagnation to movement, from narrow thinking to expansive discovery.

Stepping into new ways of thinking means loosening our grip on certainty and leaning into curiosity. It means trusting the process, allowing ourselves to be surprised, and embracing growth that doesn't fit neatly into our plans. When we let curiosity lead, we break free from limiting mindsets and open ourselves to unexpected possibilities.

The Dance Between Certainty and Curiosity

Certainty and curiosity are not entirely opposed; they exist on a spectrum. Certainty gives us a foundation to build upon, but too much attachment to it can cause us to miss opportunities. The real transformation happens in the dance between the two—the willingness to let go of rigid beliefs, even just a little, and invite curiosity in. This dance requires courage to embrace the unknown, live the questions, and trust that in doing so, new answers, perspectives, and ways of being will emerge.

In this chapter, we are called to recognize the shackles of certainty that hold us back and cultivate the curiosity that moves us forward. Growth doesn't happen in the safety of what we know but in the adventure of discovery.

What Science Has to Say

Research confirms that a growth mindset—the belief that intelligence and abilities can develop through effort—leads to greater achievement and resilience. People with a growth mindset embrace challenges, persist through obstacles, and learn from criticism. Those with a fixed mindset, believing their abilities are static, often stagnate, avoiding challenges and giving up when faced with difficulties.

Neuroscience reveals that the brain remains adaptable throughout life. This neuroplasticity—the brain's ability to form new connections—means we can continue learning and evolving well into adulthood. The way we approach uncertainty matters: Fear often pushes us into avoidance, but curiosity activates the brain's reward system, turning uncertainty into an opportunity for exploration rather than a threat.

Developmental psychology offers further insight. Erik Erikson described midlife as a stage of generativity versus stagnation. Generativity is about contributing, making a lasting impact, and remaining engaged in growth. Stagnation happens when curiosity fades, leading to a loss of purpose. Studies on positive aging confirm that those who stay open to new experiences report greater satisfaction, resilience, and mental well-being.

The evidence is clear: Adopting a growth mindset and remaining flexible are not just useful in youth; they are essential for thriving across the lifespan.

Shifts That Open Us to Possibility

Stop saying, "I can't," and start asking, "What if?": A fixed mindset says, "I can't do this." A growth mindset asks, "What if I could?" This isn't blind optimism but recognizing that with effort, learning, and the right mindset, we can develop our abilities and grow.

Run toward the challenge, not away from it: Challenges are opportunities to stretch and grow. A growth mindset leans into discomfort, knowing that growth happens outside our comfort zone.

Fail fast, learn faster: Failure isn't proof that we're not good enough; it's feedback. Instead of seeing failure as a dead end, we can view it as a teacher, asking, "What can I learn from this?"

Be open to what's next: Growth is the ongoing practice of learning, evolving, and expanding into our potential. There is always more to discover, more to refine, and more to become.

Drop the ego and pick up a notebook: Believing we already know enough limits us. True wisdom comes from being open to learning and remaining curious about what we don't yet understand.

Let the mystery be the teacher: Life is rarely black and white. Embracing complexity leads to deeper understanding, richer experiences, and more meaningful connections.

Create something that outlives you: Rather than maintaining the status quo, we can seek to create, contribute, and leave a lasting impact. Growth is more than self-improvement; it's adding value to the world.

Practical Steps for Moving from a Fixed to a Growth Mindset

Spot and challenge limiting beliefs: Recognize when your inner voice is limiting you. When you catch yourself thinking, "I'm just not good at that," pause and ask, "Is this belief helping me grow?"

Lean into challenges: Instead of seeing challenges as threats, see them as fuel for growth. True learning happens when we engage fully with discomfort.

Redefine failure as learning: Failure isn't the end; it's part of the process. Each setback is an opportunity to learn, adjust, and move forward.

Surround yourself with growth-oriented people: Your environment shapes your mindset. Seek out people who are curious, resilient, and continuously learning.

Adopt a "not yet" attitude: Instead of, "I can't do this," try, "I can't do this yet." This small shift keeps the focus on progress rather than limitation.

Celebrate small wins: Growth is not a finish line. It is the road itself. It is the small steps, the quiet shifts, and the moments that stretch you in ways you did not expect. It is paying attention, recognizing how far you have come, and staying open to what is still unfolding.

Ask, "What if?": "What if?" is a game-changer. It cracks open new possibilities and invites us to reconsider what's possible. What if you allowed yourself to explore, to wonder, and to imagine something beyond what you currently see?

What if the Question Is the Way Forward?

The world needs more people willing to live in the questions rather than settle for comfortable answers. What if the best things in your life, the ones that will stretch you, shape you, and make you more fully alive, are just outside the edges of what you think you know? What if the next chapter is not for figuring everything out but for stepping into the mystery with open hands, open eyes, and an open heart?

What if it all begins with a single question?

TL;DR

- Clinging to certainty can become a cage, preventing growth and stifling creativity.

- Curiosity is the key that unlocks the cage of certainty, allowing you to explore new possibilities and perspectives.

- Flexibility is essential for growth. Being open to change and new information helps you navigate life's challenges effectively.

- Reframe failure as a necessary part of growth. Every setback is an opportunity to learn and improve.
- True transformation happens when you step into the unknown, trust the process, and live differently, not just think differently.

PAUSE & REFLECT

- Where in your life are you clinging to certainty, and how might this be holding you back from growth?
- How can you cultivate more curiosity in your daily life and embrace the unknown with a sense of wonder?
- What recent failures have you experienced, and what lessons can you draw from them to move forward?
- In what areas could you benefit from being more flexible and open to change?
- How can you begin living into new ways of thinking, rather than just planning for change in your mind?

10

SHIFT INTO CONNECTION
YOU AREN'T MEANT TO DO THIS ALONE

*Humility is not thinking less of yourself,
it is thinking of yourself less.*
RICK WARREN

Beyond the Mirror

I used to think the world was
a place you molded
to fit the shape of your dreams.
Then I realized
the world isn't here to be conquered—
it's here to be explored.
One day,
I stopped looking in the mirror,
stopped trying to figure out who I was,

and instead,
I looked out the window.
There was a whole world out there—
messy, wild, beautiful.
And I knew
I had to go.
Not to escape myself,
but to meet myself
in unfamiliar places,
in the faces of those I hadn't yet known,
in the stories waiting to unfold.
I left behind the story,
the one where I was the hero,
and started living one
where I'm just one part of something much bigger.
Because beyond myself,
there's a world waiting to unfold,
rich with messes and marvels
and all shades in between.

THE BEST MOMENTS in life are rarely solitary. Think about the last time you felt truly happy. Odds are it wasn't when you were lost in your own thoughts or doom scrolling but when you were sharing a laugh, lending a hand, or feeling truly seen. Human connection isn't just nice to have—it's essential.

Research shows that strong relationships increase happiness, reduce stress, improve health, and even extend lifespan. Connection isn't just emotional; it's biological. Our brains and bodies are wired to thrive in relationships, and when we engage with others in meaningful ways, we experience deeper fulfillment, greater resilience, and a stronger sense of purpose.

But while we crave connection, modern life often pulls us inward. We're encouraged to focus on personal achievement, self-optimization, and independence—yet too much self-focus leaves us isolated and unfulfilled. The Dalai Lama puts it plainly: "The more time you spend thinking about yourself, the more suffering you will experience." An outward mindset—one that prioritizes relationships, contribution, and collective well-being—is the key to a richer, more satisfying life.

The Arbinger Institute has spent decades helping individuals, teams, and organizations shift from an inward to an outward mindset. Their work is built on a simple but profound idea: When we focus only on ourselves—our needs, our goals, our challenges—we limit our potential and fracture our relationships. But when we look outward, when we truly see others as people rather than as obstacles, competitors, or tools for our own success, everything changes. Arbinger's research shows that adopting an outward mindset improves collaboration, reduces conflict, and strengthens performance—whether in families, workplaces, or entire communities. Their approach has transformed organizations worldwide, from Fortune 500 companies to healthcare systems, law enforcement agencies, and even national governments.

It's more than a theory; it's a movement toward recognizing shared humanity, leading with empathy, and creating cultures where everyone thrives. Because when we see people as people—each carrying their own dreams, struggles, and aspirations—we don't just improve our relationships. We build better teams, stronger communities, and a more connected, resilient world.

Why Connection Is the Foundation of Fulfillment

It makes us happier: Harvard's eighty-five-year-long Study of Adult Development found that the quality of our relationships is the single strongest predictor of long-term happiness. It's not wealth, fame, or personal achievement—it's the people we love and who love us back. When we invest in others—through kindness, generosity, and shared experiences—we unlock a deep and lasting joy that self-focused pursuits simply can't provide.

It improves our health: Human connection isn't just good for the heart metaphorically—it's good for it literally. Research from the American Psychological Association shows that people with strong social ties have lower blood pressure, reduced risk of heart disease, and stronger immune systems. Acts of generosity, volunteering, and social bonding release oxytocin (the "love hormone"), which reduces stress and inflammation. Simply put, helping others helps us heal.

It builds resilience in hard times: Psychologist Shelley Taylor coined the phrase "tend and befriend" to describe how, in moments of crisis, humans don't just fight or flee; we seek connection. People who maintain strong relationships during difficult times experience less anxiety, quicker recovery from setbacks, and a greater sense of stability. When life hits hard, an outward mindset acts as an emotional anchor—not because we ignore our struggles, but because we don't have to face them alone.

It strengthens purpose and meaning: Ever notice how life feels more meaningful when you're engaged with something beyond yourself? Whether through mentorship, parenting, community service, or supporting a friend, investing in others amplifies our own sense of purpose. Simon Sinek puts it best: "The value of our lives is not determined by what we do for ourselves. The value of our lives is determined by what we do for others." A me-centered mindset often leaves us restless and unsatisfied. A we-centered mindset grounds us in something larger, making life richer and more meaningful.

From Me to We: The Mindset Shifts That Strengthen Connection

The quality of our lives is defined by the quality of our relationships. We thrive when we are connected—when we belong, when we contribute, when we feel seen and valued. But in a world that often rewards self-sufficiency and independence, it's easy to believe that going it alone is the ultimate goal. Yet, research—and experience—tells us otherwise. The people who lead the most fulfilling lives aren't the ones who isolate themselves in pursuit of personal success. They're the ones who invest in others, who build strong relationships, and who understand that life is better when shared. These shifts in thinking challenge the myth of self-reliance and invite us to embrace an outward mindset—one that prioritizes trust, generosity, and shared success. When we lean into connection, we don't just strengthen our relationships; we create a life that is richer, more meaningful, and deeply aligned with who we are meant to be.

You can't do it alone—and you're not supposed to: Independence is valuable, but self-sufficiency has its limits. We aren't wired to go it alone. Studies show that strong relationships protect against stress, improve mental health, and even extend lifespan. True strength is knowing when to lean in, when to ask for help, and when to open up.

The most successful people think beyond themselves: When we shift our focus from personal gain to collective well-being, we unlock the power of belonging, collaboration, and shared success. Life is richer when we stop measuring value in what we get and start asking how we contribute.

Great relationships are built on trust, not transactions: The best relationships aren't transactions—they're built on trust, care, and generosity. When we focus on what we can give, relationships deepen, bonds strengthen, and we create the kind of connections that last.

Abundance is a mindset—and it changes everything: Scarcity thinking makes us feel like we have to compete for

The best relationships aren't found. They're built— **one small act of kindness at a time.**

time, love, success, and belonging. But when we embrace abundance, we see that lifting others up doesn't diminish our own joy; it expands it. There is more than enough kindness, opportunity, and connection to go around.

Courage comes alive in connection: We often assume that burdens are ours to carry alone. But vulnerability isn't weakness; it's how we build trust. When we let others in and are honest about our struggles, we lighten the load and create space for real connection.

Success means nothing if we don't share it: No one achieves anything truly meaningful alone. Every milestone, every achievement is built on support, encouragement, and shared effort. When we acknowledge this, we stop seeing success as an individual pursuit and start seeing it as a collective journey.

How to Get Started: Simple Shifts That Strengthen Connection

Small shifts create big change. Here's how to start living with a more outward mindset, one choice at a time.

Start small—kindness goes a long way: Connection doesn't have to be grand or complicated. A warm smile, a compliment, a genuine thank you—these simple gestures signal belonging, build trust, and lift both the giver and the receiver. Research shows that small acts of kindness release oxytocin, reduce stress, and strengthen relationships. The best part? Kindness is contagious. One moment of generosity can create a ripple effect, inspiring others to do the same.

Listen like you mean it: Most of us don't listen to understand; we listen to respond. But real connection happens when we're fully present and we listen with curiosity, not an agenda. Try this: Next time someone is talking, resist the urge to jump in with advice or your own story. Instead, ask a follow-up question. Make the other person feel heard. You'll be surprised at how much deeper your relationships become.

Stop keeping score—give without expecting: We've all experienced relationships that feel like a transaction—where every favor, text, or invitation is mentally tracked. But the strongest relationships thrive on mutual generosity and trust. Instead of asking, "What can I get?" start asking, "How can I contribute?" Whether it's offering help, sharing knowledge, or simply being there, giving freely strengthens our bonds and makes connection feel effortless.

Make reflection a habit: Connection is not just a passing moment. It is the pattern we create, the way we keep showing up, and the steady rhythm of being there over time. At the end of each day, take a minute to ask, "How did I show up for others today?" Did you make someone feel valued? Did you take time to listen? Did you express gratitude? Reflection keeps us accountable to the kind of person we want to be.

Put your phone down and look up: Want to instantly improve your connections? Be where you are. Make eye contact. Put your phone away when talking to someone. Give your full attention to the moment in front of you. People can feel when we're fully present, and that presence creates deeper, more meaningful interactions.

Choose collaboration over comparison: It's easy to see life as a competition—who's more successful, who's getting ahead. But comparison breeds disconnection. Collaboration, on the other hand, brings people together. Celebrate others' wins. Offer support without hesitation. The more we choose "we" over "me," the more we realize that success is richer when it's shared.

Show up consistently, not just when it's convenient: Strong relationships aren't built in one big moment; they're built in the small, consistent choices we make every day. Send the text. Make the call. Check in. Show up for the people in your life, even when there's nothing in it for you. Trust and connection grow when people know you'll be there, and not just when it's easy, but when it matters most.

How to Create More "We" Moments

Small shifts in how we engage with others can create big ripples of connection. Here are more ways to step out of isolation and into meaningful relationships.

Make the first move: Don't wait for someone else to reach out—send the text, make the call, or invite someone to coffee. Connection starts with showing up.

Be the person who remembers: Birthdays, big milestones, even small wins—acknowledge them. A simple "Thinking of you" can mean more than you realize.

Turn daily routines into social moments: Grab a workout buddy, cook dinner with family, or have a standing coffee date with a friend.

Practice micro-connections: Chat with the barista, ask your neighbor how they're doing, or say hello to a stranger. Small connections remind us we're part of something bigger.

Surprise someone with kindness: Write a note of appreciation, bring a colleague their favorite coffee, or help out without being asked. Unexpected generosity deepens bonds.

Prioritize face-to-face over digital: Whenever possible, choose an in-person meetup over a text. Human connection thrives on eye contact, laughter, and shared presence.

Find shared purpose: Join a book club, volunteer together, or work on a project with a friend. Collaboration strengthens connection.

End the day with gratitude: Before bed, reflect on the people who made a difference in your day—and tell them.

Gratitude isn't just feeling thankful; it requires expressing it.

The key to connection? Intention: The more we create these moments, the more we build a life filled with meaning, belonging, and community. The more we shift from "me" to "we," the more we thrive.

Why This Matters: The Big Picture

Midlife has a way of forcing us to take stock. The things that once kept us busy—careers, raising kids, chasing achievement—start to shift. Some of the noise quiets, and in that space, a question emerges: What really matters now?

Here's the answer, plain and simple: relationships.

Yet, this is also the stage where connection can slip through the cracks. The kids don't need us in the same way. Friends are juggling their own responsibilities. Work isn't the all-consuming force it once was. If we're not intentional, we can wake up one day and realize we're more isolated than we ever expected.

But midlife isn't the time to retreat; it's the time to re-engage. To double down on the relationships that energize us. To seek out new ones. To build a life where we don't just go through the motions but actually enjoy the people we're doing life with.

In our communities, trust and mutual support create a stronger sense of belonging, deeper friendships, and a better quality of life. When we reach out, check in, and make time for the people around us, we create the kind of environment where everyone thrives.

In our personal lives, connection is a necessity. Research shows that strong relationships are as critical to our health as diet and exercise. The more we invest in others, the more purpose and fulfillment we feel in return. And generosity? It's not a sacrifice; it's a strategy. The more we give, the more we build the kind of relationships that sustain us.

So, what's next? What's one small step you can take today to shift from "me" to "we"? A quick check-in. A conversation that goes beyond surface level. A moment of encouragement—with no agenda, no expectation. These moments aren't just nice gestures. They're the foundation of a meaningful second half of life. And in the end, isn't that what we're really after?

TL;DR

- Midlife is a turning point. The roles and priorities that once defined us start to shift, making connection more important than ever.

- We aren't meant to go it alone. Research confirms that strong relationships increase happiness, resilience, and even longevity.

- An outward mindset enriches our lives. When we focus on what we can give rather than what we can get, we create stronger, more fulfilling relationships.

- Small moments of connection matter. A kind word, a deep conversation, or simply being present can transform relationships.

- Generosity is a strategy, not a sacrifice. Giving to others builds the kind of relationship that sustains us and creates a sense of purpose.

- Collaboration beats comparison. Life is richer when we celebrate each other's wins and support one another instead of competing.

- Success means nothing if we don't share it. The most meaningful moments in life are those we experience together.

PAUSE & REFLECT

- Who are the people in your life who energize and support you? How often do you make time for them?
- When was the last time you reached out to someone just because? What's stopping you from doing it more?
- If connection is as essential as diet and exercise, how are you "feeding" your relationships?
- What's one small action you can take today to move from "me" to "we"?
- What kind of relationships do you want to cultivate in this next phase of life? What will it take to make that happen?

11

SHIFT INTO RESPONSE-ABILITY
THE PAUSE THAT CHANGES THINGS

Emotions are like waves. You can't stop them from coming,
but you can choose which ones to surf.
JONATAN MÅRTENSSON

The Pause
There's a moment,
right there,
between what happens to you
and what you do with it.
It's a sliver of time,
a heartbeat,
barely noticeable

unless you're looking for it.
But oh,
that pause—
it's everything.
It's the place
where you're not a puppet
on the strings of circumstance.
It's where you realize
you have a choice,
where you can breathe,
where you can decide
who you want to be.
In that pause,
you're not reacting,
you're creating.
You're stepping into the space
where freedom lives,
where possibility thrives.
The world may rush on,
a blur of demands and noise,
but here,
in this pause,
you're guiding,
you're free,
you're powerful.
Step into the pause.
Honor it.
Don't rush past it.
Let it breathe.
In that space,
you uncover

a version of you
that sees differently
and acts with new eyes.
And that,
that changes everything.

EMOTIONS SHAPE EVERYTHING. Every decision, every conversation, every action. Whether we realize it or not, they're driving the bus, fueling our behavior, influencing our relationships, and shaping the way we lead. And understanding them isn't some side project. It's the work.

Daniel Goleman, the pioneer of emotional intelligence, has spent years proving that how we manage our emotions matters just as much as, maybe even more than, IQ when it comes to success. Brené Brown shows us that vulnerability isn't weakness; it's the path to deeper connection and creativity. And Viktor Frankl, a Holocaust survivor and psychiatrist, spoke to the power of meaning, resilience, and choice. Even in unimaginable suffering, there is still agency, still a way to decide who we will be.

Between what happens and how we respond, there's room for pause. And in that pause? That's where it all shifts. That's where we get to choose. Not just a reaction, but a posture, a perspective, a meaning. That pause is freedom. That pause is power. That pause is where growth happens.

Emotional regulation lives in that space: the ability to pause before reacting, to notice what's rising up, and to decide, with clarity, what happens next. Not pushing emotions away. Not letting them take over. But working with them, learning from them, and moving through them with intention.

I didn't coin the term "response-ability," but I've come to really value what it represents—the quiet, courageous act of choosing how we show up to what life hands us. Our response-ability is the inner strength to stay present with what is happening and to choose a response that reflects our values, clarity, and growth. It begins with awareness. You notice what's rising in you, what's pulling at you, and what the moment is asking of you. And then you respond—not from impulse, but from alignment.

Like any meaningful practice, response-ability deepens over time. It grows through repetition—through small, everyday choices. The more you return to it, the more it becomes part of you. The space between what happens and how you respond begins to feel less like a gap and more like a gift—a place of agency, creativity, and grounded presence.

Response-ability shapes how you lead yourself. It brings your whole self—body, mind, heart, and soul—into the room. It invites you to show up with presence, not perfection. And from that place, you move with integrity, build trust, and become someone who can hold the weight of the moment and still act with grace.

This is how we change. Not all at once. But moment by moment, response by response, choosing to stay present and respond with care.

Emotional Regulation in Practice

What does emotional regulation actually look like in real life? It's choosing to listen instead of lashing out. It's pausing before reacting in a tense meeting. It's recognizing frustration without letting it dictate our words or actions. It's the difference between reacting on impulse and responding with clarity and purpose.

Emotional regulation is learning to stay steady when everything around you pulls for a reaction. It is showing up with clarity, adjusting, growing, and responding in ways that reflect what matters most. Leaders who develop it build stronger teams. Parents who practice it deepen their relationships with their kids. Friends who lean into it create trust instead of tension. It is the work of paying attention, staying present, and choosing how to move forward.

We like to think we're logical, rational beings. That we make calculated decisions based purely on reason. But the truth? Emotions drive most of our choices. Even the most analytical, data-driven people are motivated by emotions. The desire for control? That's emotional. The need for certainty? Emotional. The drive for success? Emotional. Our brains interpret experiences through a filter of emotions, past experiences, and subconscious biases. Ignoring that just makes us blind to what's really influencing us. Once we accept that emotions are at play, we can learn to work with them instead of being ruled by them.

Between what happens and how you respond, there is a space. **That space is your freedom.**

What Science Says About Emotional Regulation

Emotional regulation is a game-changer for well-being and performance. Here's what research tells us.

Changing how you think changes how you feel: Cognitive reappraisal—a fancy term for reframing a situation—helps us shift our emotional response. The more we practice this, the better we get at reducing stress and increasing positive emotions.

Your mental health depends on it: People who suppress or ruminate on emotions are more prone to anxiety and depression. Those who practice healthy regulation strategies—like reappraising situations, problem-solving, or even just talking things out—handle challenges more effectively.

It's good for your body too: Better emotional regulation is linked to lower inflammation, which reduces the risk of chronic illnesses like heart disease and diabetes.

Your brain gets better at it over time: Regularly practicing emotional regulation strengthens neural pathways that support resilience. Every time you choose to regulate rather than react, you're reinforcing healthier patterns.

What Experts Have to Say

Lisa Feldman Barrett: Barrett, a leading neuroscientist, argues that emotions aren't just automatic reactions; they're constructed based on past experiences and present circumstances. This means we have more control over them than we think.

James Gross: A psychology professor at Stanford, Gross studies cognitive reappraisal and how changing our thoughts can change our emotions. This is a practical, everyday tool for managing stress and rethinking challenges as opportunities.

Stephen Porges: Porges's Polyvagal Theory highlights the link between emotional regulation and our sense of safety. When we feel secure, we manage emotions better. Creating environments where people feel safe—at work, at home, or in relationships—is crucial.

Jon Kabat-Zinn: The founder of mindfulness-based stress reduction, Kabat-Zinn teaches that mindfulness—paying attention to emotions without judgment—helps reduce reactivity and promotes clarity.

Richard Davidson: A psychology and psychiatry professor, Davidson is known for research on neuroplasticity that shows that practices like meditation can rewire the brain to handle emotions more effectively over time.

The Will Smith Slap

If you need proof of the power of emotional regulation, consider a moment many of us witnessed: Will Smith, one of the most respected actors of his generation, reacting in real time to a joke that hit too close to home. In response to a comment Chris Rock made about Smith's wife Jada Pinkett Smith at the 2022 Oscars, Smith slapped Rock on stage and on live television. In a flash, what could have been handled privately became a viral controversy—one that reshaped his career, damaged his reputation, and eclipsed what should have been a defining moment of celebration. Whether or not you believe it was staged, the impact was undeniable. One choice, made in a split-second, became the headline.

That's the space emotional regulation gives us—the pause before the reaction, the breath that can change the outcome. It's in that space where we find our ability to choose, stay aligned, and lead ourselves in a way we won't have to explain away later. Because one moment can change everything.

Exploring Mindsets Around Emotional Regulation

Let's take a closer look at the mindsets that shape how we handle our emotions—both the helpful ones that empower us and the unhelpful ones that hold us back. Our ability to harness our emotions is influenced by the way we think about them, so let's explore some perspectives that can either steer us toward growth or keep us stuck in patterns that don't serve us.

Helpful Mindsets

Learning to regulate emotions is more than a skill. It's a way of navigating the human experience with awareness and intention. It's paying attention to what's happening inside, understanding that emotions aren't just reactions;

they're messages, signals guiding us toward a fuller life. Here are some ways to start seeing emotional regulation as something that deepens relationships, strengthens resilience, and grounds you in who you truly are.

Emotions are data—use them wisely: Your emotions aren't obstacles; they're information. They're signals that point you toward what truly matters—your needs, values, and aspirations. When you stop seeing emotions as distractions and start recognizing them as valuable data, you gain the ability to respond with intention instead of reacting out of habit.

The power to choose is the power to lead myself: You may not control every situation, but you always control how you respond. Between every trigger and your reaction, there is a moment of choice. That space is where self-leadership lives. The strongest leaders—whether in business, relationships, or personal growth—are the ones who use that space to align their actions with their values.

Trust is built in the moments between emotion and reaction: Emotional regulation isn't suppressing feelings; it's channeling them in a way that builds trust. When you manage your emotions effectively, you communicate with clarity, avoid unnecessary conflict, and create space for others to feel seen and heard. Relationships—whether personal or professional—thrive when we make intentional choices about how we show up.

Emotional strength is a skill, not a trait: No one is born with perfect emotional regulation. It's a muscle that gets stronger with practice. Every challenge—every moment of frustration, anger, or excitement—is an opportunity to refine that skill. The people who lead with emotional intelligence aren't special; they're just committed to the work.

Self-awareness is the foundation of great leadership: If emotional regulation is the skill, self-awareness is the foundation. People who lead themselves well pay attention to what they're feeling and why. They know that emotional intelligence isn't about avoiding emotions but understanding them so they can make better decisions.

A pause is the difference between reaction and impact: A single pause can change everything. The ability to step back, take a breath, and assess before responding is what separates great leaders from those who let emotions dictate their actions. A pause isn't weakness; it's the gateway to making decisions that align with who you are and what you stand for.

Emotional regulation fuels resilience and longevity: Resilience is about navigating hardship with intention. The most enduring leaders, teams, and relationships aren't the ones that never experience difficulty. They're the ones that know how to regulate their emotions in the face of challenge. Emotional intelligence is what makes resilience sustainable.

Unhelpful Mindsets

Emotional regulation is one of the hardest things we'll ever do—not because it's complicated, but because it requires deep self-awareness, discipline, and practice. It's the difference between reacting and responding, between letting emotions drive the moment and using them as a tool for clarity and connection.

But here's the problem: Most of us have picked up unhelpful mindsets along the way—beliefs about emotions that limit our ability to manage them effectively. We've been taught that certain emotions are bad, that controlling our reactions is a personality trait rather than a skill, or that other people are responsible for how we feel. And these beliefs don't just shape how we experience emotions; they shape how we show up in the world. If we want to lead better—at work, in relationships, and in life—we need to challenge these unhelpful mindsets. Let's take a closer look at the ones that might be holding us back.

Suppressing my emotions will make them go away: Many people believe that pushing emotions down is the best way to stay in control. But suppression isn't control; it's just delay. The emotions fester and show up later as stress, anxiety, or explosive reactions that feel out of proportion. Rather than bottle things up, the strongest people are the ones who understand their emotions and channel them productively.

My emotions control me: If you believe this, you're giving up your agency. When emotions dictate every reaction, life feels like it's happening *to* you instead of *because of* you. But emotions aren't in control—you are. The moment you recognize that emotions are signals, not orders, you reclaim your ability to respond with intention rather than impulse.

Only naturally calm people can regulate their emotions: Some people assume that emotional regulation is a trait—something you're born with. If you're naturally fiery, passionate, or high-energy, you might think it's just not in you to stay composed. That's simply not true. Emotional regulation is a skill, and skills can be learned. No matter your personality, you can develop the ability to manage emotions effectively. The goal isn't to stay calm for the sake of calm. It's to be clear, decisive, and intentional—showing up in a way that aligns with what matters most.

I can't change how I feel: Believing that your emotions are permanent is one of the biggest barriers to growth. If you think your feelings are fixed, then you don't see the point in trying to manage them. But emotions are fluid. They're shaped by your thoughts, your actions, and your mindset. You *can* change how you feel—not by force, but by choice.

Reacting quickly makes me strong: Many people confuse impulsiveness with strength. They believe that quick reactions show confidence and decisiveness. But the truth is, most of our worst decisions come from acting too fast. Strength isn't about reacting in the moment; it's about having the discipline to pause, assess, and respond with clarity. Leaders who take their time make better choices, and better choices build trust.

Other people are responsible for my emotions: If you believe this, you're handing over your power. When you think someone else *made* you angry or *caused* your frustration, you give them control over your inner world. The truth is, emotions start and end with you. You can't control what others do, but you can *always* control how you respond. Emotional regulation begins when you stop blaming and start owning.

Emotional regulation means suppressing how I feel: There's a dangerous belief that managing emotions means hiding them. That's not regulation; it's avoidance. The goal isn't to pretend emotions don't exist, but to express them in a way that is clear, constructive, and aligned with who you want to be. Rather than shutting emotions down, true regulation is learning to hold them, listen to them, and let them pass through without taking over.

I'll never be good at emotional regulation: When you tell yourself that emotional regulation is beyond you, you lock yourself into old patterns. You assume that how you've always reacted is how you *have* to react. But that's not how growth works. Emotional regulation is something you build. With practice, anyone can develop it. And the more you do, the more control you gain—not just over your emotions, but over the life you're creating.

Practical Strategies for Emotional Regulation in Midlife

Midlife is a season of change. Roles shift, priorities evolve, and emotions often run high. Whether you're navigating career transitions, caring for aging parents, or redefining personal goals, emotional regulation becomes one of the most powerful skills you can develop. You don't have to suppress your emotions. You just need to lead yourself through them with clarity and purpose. Here's how.

Use the power of the pause: Before reacting, pause. Take a deep breath. Count to three. This small moment of space allows you to respond rather than react. In midlife, when stakes feel higher—whether in relationships, career, or health—this practice can mean the difference between a knee-jerk reaction and a decision aligned with your values.

Reframe the story you're telling yourself: Your perspective shapes your reality. When your adult child makes a decision you wouldn't have made, do you see it as a rejection of your guidance or as a sign they're learning to stand on their own? When they don't call as often, do you assume they don't care or do you recognize that they're navigating their own season of growth? Reframing your story shifts your emotional state and gives you control over your response.

Practice mindfulness to stay present: In midlife, it's easy to get caught up in what's next or dwell on what could have been. Mindfulness helps you stay present. This is not a fight to eliminate emotions. It is learning to recognize them, see them for what they are, and choose your response instead of letting them take the lead.

Move your body to reset your mind: Physical activity is more than fitness. It is a way to manage stress, lift your mood, and build resilience. A walk, a workout, or a simple stretch can reset your nervous system, bringing clarity and helping you move through the day with focus and energy.

Write it down to gain perspective: Journaling is a tool for clarity. Writing down your thoughts helps you process emotions, recognize patterns in your reactions, and gain insights into what truly matters at this stage of life. Sometimes, the act of putting words on paper is enough to shift your mindset.

Set boundaries to protect your energy: Midlife often brings the realization that time and energy are finite. Not every situation or person deserves your full emotional investment. Learning when to say no and where to step back isn't avoidance but self-respect. Boundaries allow you to focus on what truly matters.

Give yourself grace: Emotional regulation is a lifelong practice. Frustration will come. Overwhelm will come. Impatience will come. But what matters is how you meet those moments—whether you let them sweep you away or take a breath, steady yourself, and choose what happens next.

Emotions are data, not directives. They tell you something, but they don't have to drive the bus.

The Power of Speaking It Out Loud

We often assume that emotional regulation is something we have to figure out on our own. That if we just try harder, think our way through it, or suppress what we feel, we'll gain control. But sometimes, the most powerful step in managing emotions isn't solving them. It's saying them out loud.

I regularly hear breakthrough stories from the counselors on our team: people who have wrestled with the same emotional patterns for years, only to find clarity and relief by simply naming their struggles in a safe space. Therapy is not a repair job. It is a doorway. A chance to see yourself with fresh eyes, to understand the patterns that have shaped you, and to step into a new way of being—one that feels truer, freer, and more fully your own.

Let's Talk About Therapy

There are seasons in life when emotions feel overwhelming, steering us away from the life we truly want. When we find ourselves stuck—unable to make choices that align with our values or feeling disconnected in our relationships—it might be time for extra support.

Therapy can be a game-changer for emotional regulation, especially when our usual ways of coping aren't enough. When emotions like anxiety, anger, or sadness seem to take control, therapy offers a space to explore what's really going on beneath the surface. It helps us uncover the patterns that keep us stuck, understand why certain emotions hold so much power, and learn new strategies for managing them effectively.

One of the biggest benefits of therapy is the perspective it provides. We get so close to our own struggles that it's hard to see them clearly. A therapist helps us step back, challenge unhelpful mindsets, and shift emotional patterns so we can make decisions that truly align with who we are.

Therapy isn't just for what's happening right now. It's laying the groundwork, strengthening the core, and shaping how we step into what's next. Learning to regulate emotions changes everything: how we connect, how we decide, and how we move through the world with steadiness and resilience.

If you've ever hesitated to try therapy because of old stereotypes or misconceptions, I encourage you to challenge those beliefs. Therapy is not a sign of weakness. It is a space for learning, growing, and stepping into a deeper understanding of yourself. It is where clarity takes root and where real change begins.

Internal Family Systems: A Rising Star in Emotional Regulation

If you've ever felt like your emotions have a mind of their own, that's because, in a way, they do. That's the core idea behind Internal Family Systems (IFS), a therapeutic approach that has become increasingly recognized as a powerful tool for emotional regulation and personal growth. IFS sees the mind not as one unified voice but as a community of "parts": inner voices or subpersonalities, each with its own perspective, emotional tone, and purpose. You might have a part that's fiercely protective, a part that carries pain from the past, a part that's driven to succeed, and another that just wants to be left alone. These parts are not problems to fix but aspects of you that developed to help you navigate life—especially the rough patches.

The goal of IFS is to build a compassionate relationship with these inner parts. Instead of trying to silence, suppress, or override them, you learn to listen with curiosity. What is this part trying to protect me from? What does it need? By getting to know these internal voices, you start to create space between the emotion and the reaction. That space is where self-leadership begins.

In IFS, there's also the concept of the Self—your core, grounded inner presence. The Self is calm, curious, compassionate, and clear. It's not a part; it's the leader within. When you lead your internal system from Self, you're no longer at the mercy of your parts. You're in relationship with them. You can hear the inner critic, feel the anxiety, notice the pain—and respond with steadiness instead of being swept away.

This is what makes IFS a deeply practical model for self-leadership. It teaches you how to hold space for your full emotional experience without letting any one part hijack the whole system. Over time, that ability—to pause, listen, and lead from Self—builds resilience, clarity, and real inner confidence.

The research backs it up. IFS has been shown to reduce symptoms of anxiety, depression, and post-traumatic stress disorder. But perhaps even more powerfully, it offers a way to feel more whole and lead your inner life with the same grace and clarity you'd want from any great leader—only this time, that leader is you.

Emotional Regulation Is Your Midlife Advantage

Midlife is a season of transition. It's a time when old patterns either serve us or hold us back. Emotional regulation is the key to navigating these shifts with wisdom and clarity. It's what allows us to lead ourselves instead of being led by the emotions of the moment. Whether through therapy, tools like IFS, or intentional daily practices, emotional regulation is a superpower. It helps us strengthen relationships, make better decisions, and approach life's changes with confidence.

And the best part? You don't have to figure it all out overnight. You just have to start. One moment of self-awareness. One pause before reacting. One intentional decision at a time. Because the ability to regulate your emotions isn't just about feeling better. It's about living better.

TL;DR

- Emotions are signals, not problems. Learning to interpret them instead of suppressing them leads to better decision-making.

- The pause is your power. A split second between stimulus and response can change everything.

- Reframing shifts your emotional state. The story you tell yourself about a situation determines how you feel about it.

- Movement matters. Physical activity isn't just for fitness—it's one of the most effective ways to regulate emotions.

- Boundaries protect your energy. Not every person or situation deserves your emotional investment.

- Therapy is much more than fixing. It's a process of understanding. Saying something out loud can be the breakthrough that shifts everything.

- Internal Family Systems helps you lead your emotions so you aren't led by them instead. Understanding your emotional "parts" creates harmony and self-awareness.

- Emotional regulation isn't about being perfect; it's about being intentional. One choice at a time is enough.

PAUSE & REFLECT

- What's one emotional habit you've been carrying for years that might not be serving you anymore?
- When you feel overwhelmed, do you tend to shut down, lash out, or distract yourself? What would it look like to handle it differently?
- If your emotions had a voice, what would they be trying to tell you that you haven't been willing to hear?
- What's one situation in your life right now where pausing before reacting could make all the difference?
- If you could offer yourself the same compassion you give to a close friend, what would you say to yourself about how you handle emotions?

12

SHIFT INTO ALIGNMENT
SYNC WITH WHAT MATTERS

In order to live in the world as reflective beings, humans seem to need three things: They need to comprehend the world around them, they need to find direction for their actions, and they need to find worth in their lives.
FRANK MARTELA AND MICHAEL STEGER

Sometimes the Soul Waits

There is a part of you
that does not measure your worth
by what you've accomplished.
It does not rush you to be whole
before you are ready.
This part of you moves slowly.
Quietly.
Like morning light
across the floor.

It waits—not in hiding,
but because it knows
you'll find your way back
when you are ready
to lay it all down
and listen.
It is not asking you to be perfect.
It is not waiting for applause.
It only hopes you will notice
your outer edges
coming into focus.
And when the noise fades
and pressures subside,
you will hear it.
Not all at once;
gradually, then suddenly.
And it will say:
You made it here.
I've been waiting for you.

MEANING IN LIFE is the quiet force that guides us, the anchor that holds us steady when everything else feels uncertain. It isn't something we can measure or quantify, yet we feel its presence (or absence) deeply. Meaning is found in our connections, our experiences, and the impact we leave behind. But the irony is that we often don't recognize it when it's right in front of us. We only realize its significance when it feels out of reach. And yet, when we do grasp it, our lives become a testament to our purpose, a reflection of what truly matters.

My Morning Puzzle

Each morning, I start my day with a ritual: coffee in one hand, *New York Times* Wordle and Connections puzzles on the screen. Some days, I move through them effortlessly, convinced I've tapped into some hidden genius. Other days, I stare at the screen, wondering if I've ever understood language at all. It's a daily reminder that some things in life feel like they come naturally, while others leave us grasping for clarity.

Searching for meaning in midlife feels a lot like this. Some days, everything aligns. Other days, we wrestle with the feeling that something is just slightly *off*, like a sweater that no longer fits the way it used to. We try to make sense of it, to smooth it out, but it refuses to cooperate. Or maybe it's more like folding a fitted sheet—no matter how many times we try, we still end up with a lumpy, misshapen pile.

The mistake we often make is believing that meaning is something to *solve*, something that has a single right answer. But meaning isn't a puzzle. It's something we create, something we recognize in the process of living. The challenge isn't in finding it; it's in seeing where it already exists.

The Simplicity of Presence

What if we've been making this harder than it needs to be? What if meaning isn't something we need to chase, but something we need to notice?

There's a cultural obsession with *finding* meaning, as if it's hiding somewhere, waiting to be uncovered. But meaning isn't always a grand revelation. More often, it's in the small, everyday moments we tend to overlook—the morning light hitting the kitchen counter, the warmth of a well-brewed cup of coffee, the quiet feeling of knowing you've made someone's day just a little bit better.

These moments don't always announce themselves as meaningful. They don't arrive with a flashing sign that says, "This is it! This is what matters!" But when we slow down enough to pay attention, we realize that meaning isn't something waiting at the end of a long journey. It's woven into the fabric of our lives already.

But what if meaning wasn't built into life at all? Would that make things easier?

Existential thinkers have wrestled with this idea for centuries—the notion that life doesn't come with a preset purpose. No instruction manual, no grand design that tells us exactly what we're supposed to do. Some philosophers argue that we are, in a sense, dropped into an indifferent universe, and it's up to us to create our own meaning.

At first glance, this might seem disheartening. But if we lean into it, we might find something liberating in the idea.

The Existential Thinkers on Meaning

Søren Kierkegaard believed that meaning isn't something we find—it's something we *choose*. He famously wrote, "Life can only be understood backwards; but it must be lived forwards." We make sense of our lives by looking at where we've been, but we don't have the luxury of knowing how it will all turn out. That's why meaning requires a leap of faith—a commitment to living in alignment with what feels true and authentic, even when the path ahead is uncertain.

Jean-Paul Sartre took this a step further, arguing that "existence precedes essence." In other words, we aren't born with a fixed purpose; we define ourselves through the choices we make. This freedom to shape our own meaning is both empowering and a heavy responsibility—because if meaning isn't given to us, it means we must actively create it.

Albert Camus introduced the idea of the absurd—the clash between our deep desire for meaning and a universe that doesn't inherently provide it. In *The Myth of Sisyphus*, he imagines Sisyphus—condemned to roll a boulder up a hill for eternity—as happy, not because his task is meaningful in the traditional sense, but because he chooses to engage with it anyway. Camus's message? Meaning isn't necessarily about what we do, but about *how* we engage with life, even in the struggle.

You don't have to overhaul your life to find meaning. **You just have to notice where it already exists.**

The Paradox of a Meaningless Life

So, what happens if we fully accept that life has no inherent meaning? On one hand, there's relief—no pressure, no need to search for a singular purpose, no fear of getting it "wrong." But on the other hand, without meaning, life can feel empty. Without a sense of purpose, our actions might start to feel hollow, our relationships transactional, our efforts insignificant.

This is the paradox: Believing that life is meaningless can free us from the weight of expectation, but it can also strip away the very thing that makes life rich and fulfilling. So where does that leave us? Somewhere in the middle. The struggle to create meaning is, in itself, what makes life matter. It's in the choosing, in the effort, in the small acts of presence and engagement that add up to something far greater than the sum of their parts.

A New Way to Think About Meaning

If meaning isn't handed to us, then the real question isn't "What is the meaning of life?" It's "What makes my life feel meaningful?"

Maybe it's the work we do, the people we love, the ways we contribute to something bigger than ourselves. Maybe it's the way we show up, even when things are hard. Maybe it's simply recognizing that life, in all its unpredictability, is still full of moments worth holding onto. Whatever it is, one thing is clear: Meaning isn't something waiting for us in the future. It's something we build, right here, right now, in the way we choose to live today.

The Science of Meaning

For years, meaning has been treated as something philosophical, personal, or even spiritual. But science tells us something different. Meaning isn't just a lofty idea—it's a fundamental pillar of well-being. It shapes our mental health, our resilience, and even our longevity.

Dr. Michael Steger, a professor at Colorado State University and one of the leading researchers on meaning, has spent years studying its impact on happiness and life satisfaction. His findings are clear: When people perceive their lives as meaningful, they are happier, but they're also healthier, more resilient, and better equipped to handle life's challenges.

This isn't just about personal fulfillment; it's about survival. People who live with a sense of purpose experience lower levels of stress and anxiety, stronger relationships, and even better physical health. Meaning, it turns out, isn't a luxury. It's a necessity.

Research That Matters

The connection between meaning and overall well-being is a well-documented reality. Psychological research has consistently found that people who report a strong sense of meaning in their lives experience

- higher levels of life satisfaction and overall happiness;
- lower rates of depression and anxiety;

- greater resilience in the face of stress;
- increased engagement in health-promoting behaviors, such as exercise and social connection; and
- a stronger ability to navigate difficult life transitions.

Steger's research has been instrumental in demonstrating that meaning does more than make us feel better—it helps us *live* better. His studies show that when people feel a sense of purpose, they tend to make healthier choices, build stronger relationships, and find it easier to recover from setbacks.

Psychologists Carol Ryff and Burton Singer have reinforced these findings, showing that meaning acts as a protective factor against emotional distress. People who report high levels of meaning are less likely to feel lost during times of uncertainty and are more likely to adapt to changes with a sense of purpose.

And it doesn't stop at psychology. Emily Esfahani Smith, author of *The Power of Meaning*, has explored how a strong sense of purpose can even be a predictor of longevity. People who feel that their lives have meaning tend to live longer, healthier lives than those who don't.

This research has profound implications for midlife—because this is the season when meaning often feels most in flux. After years spent building careers, raising families, and achieving goals, many people find themselves asking, "Now what?" The external markers of success don't always feel as fulfilling as they once did, and without clear direction, it's easy to feel adrift.

But here's the encouraging part: Meaning isn't something that fades as we get older. In fact, research suggests that people often experience *greater* levels of meaning later in life as they shift from striving toward external achievements to focusing more on relationships, purpose, and legacy. Studies in positive psychology show that even when people go through significant life transitions—retirement, an empty nest, career shifts—those who cultivate a sense of meaning in their daily lives experience far less distress. Meaning acts as an anchor, providing stability even when external circumstances change.

Faith, Meaning, and the Big Questions

It's a tricky time to talk about faith. Conversations can feel loaded, divisive, and tangled up in history, politics, and personal experiences. But if you step back from the noise, if you strip away the layers of doctrine and debate, something fascinating emerges: Across different traditions, different cultures, and different belief systems, we're all wrestling with the same questions. Why are we here? What makes life matter? How do we live in a way that feels rich, deep, and true?

While the answers vary, the themes are remarkably similar. Christianity talks about "vocation"—this idea that we are called to live with purpose, not just in what we do, but in how we show up for others. Judaism speaks of "*mitzvot*"—acts of kindness and justice that ground everyday life in meaning. Islam teaches that purpose comes through "alignment"—living in harmony with divine intention. In Buddhism and Hinduism, meaning is found in "awakening"—seeing life as it truly is and learning to live with wisdom and presence. Different frameworks, different languages, but underneath it all? A shared recognition that meaning isn't something we passively receive. It's something we engage with, something we cultivate.

Maybe that's the point. Maybe it's not about whose definition of meaning is "right," but about recognizing that we're all drawn toward something bigger than ourselves. Some call it God; some call it love; some call it connection, purpose, dharma, calling. But the thread running through all of it is the same: You are here, your life matters, and what you do with it shapes the world around you. What if, instead of focusing on the differences, we paid attention to what we all seem to know deep down? That meaning isn't just found—it's made. One choice, one relationship, one act of love at a time.

It all points to a simple yet powerful truth: Meaning goes beyond personal satisfaction. It encompasses well-being on every level—mental, emotional, physical, and social. When we cultivate meaning—whether through relationships, contributions to others, or a connection to something bigger than ourselves—we're not just enriching our own lives. We're also contributing to the larger fabric of a more connected, resilient, and fulfilling world. And the best part? We don't have to wait for meaning. It's something we can cultivate, one intentional choice at a time.

Helpful Mindsets Around Meaning

The way we approach meaning shapes how we experience it. Sometimes, a small shift in perspective helps us see that meaning isn't something we have to chase—it's already here. Here are some helpful mindsets to cultivate a deeper sense of meaning in everyday life.

Meaning is in the everyday: We get this idea that meaning has to be epic, like a big, cinematic moment when the music swells, and suddenly, we understand our life's purpose. But meaning is sneaky. It hides in the small stuff. The way your friend's face lights up when you show up. The conversation that lingers in your mind for days. That quiet, contented feeling when you finally get the fitted sheet folded right (or at least close enough). Meaning isn't some far-off achievement. It's in the cup of tea you make for someone. The extra mile you go. The way you choose to show up even when you don't have to.

I create meaning through my actions: Meaning isn't something you stumble upon; it's something you shape, build, and bring into the world. It's in the way you treat people. It's in the words you choose. It's in the way you put love into what you do. Every small act of kindness, every moment of generosity, every time you decide to lean in instead of checking out—you're creating meaning. You are making the world a little more whole and a little more connected, just by choosing to engage.

Meaning is already here, not just in the future: It's easy to think meaning is somewhere out ahead of us, waiting in the next job, the next achievement, and the next big breakthrough. But what if meaning isn't focused on what's next? What if it's focused on what's *now*? What if instead of chasing meaning, we started noticing it? In our work, in our relationships, and even in the struggles that stretch us and shape us. When we stop believing that meaning is always *one step away*, we start to see that it's been showing up all along.

Relationships deepen my sense of meaning: Want to know where meaning loves to hang out? In relationships. Not just the big, defining ones, but the small, everyday connections that make life feel real. The late-night talk with a friend. The hug that lingers a second longer than expected. The way someone remembers your favorite song and plays it when you need it most. We don't find meaning alone. We find it in the spaces between us, in the give and take of relationships, and in the way we show up for each other when it matters.

Reflection helps me see what matters: Sometimes we get so caught up in doing that we forget to *notice*. To pause. To step back and ask, "What's actually making me feel alive? What's bringing me joy? What am I doing just because I think I should?" Reflection isn't overthinking; it's paying attention. And when we pay attention, we start to see patterns: what lifts us up, what weighs us down, what actually matters. From there, we can start making choices that align with what we know is meaningful.

Unhelpful Mindsets Around Meaning

Just as some mindsets open the door to meaning, others slam it shut. These are the stories we tell ourselves that keep meaning feeling just out of reach.

Meaning comes only from big achievements: We've been told that meaning is found in the big things—the dream job, the life-changing moment, or the grand achievement. But that's a trap, because if meaning is only in the big things, then what are we doing in the meantime? Just passing time until something "meaningful" finally happens? No. Meaning isn't just in the big wins. It's in the tiny, unnoticed, everyday acts of love, patience, and presence.

Meaning is always out there, just beyond reach: If we keep telling ourselves that meaning is somewhere else—somewhere we haven't gotten to yet—then we'll always be chasing, never arriving. But what if meaning isn't *out there*? What if it's in here—in how we choose to engage with today? In how we pour ourselves into whatever's in front of us, right now?

Others have more meaningful lives than I do: Comparison is the fastest way to kill your sense of meaning. When you're busy looking at what *they* have, what *they're* doing, what *their* life looks like, you miss what's unfolding right in front of you. Meaning is deeply personal. The journey isn't defined by following someone else's success. It's about finding your own purpose, embracing your unique path, and staying true to what matters most to you.

I'll focus on meaning later, when I have time: We push meaning to the back burner. We think, "I'll get to it later. When things calm down. When I have more space. When life isn't so crazy." But meaning can't be scheduled for the future. When we stop postponing meaning and step into it now, we start to see that it's been here all along, waiting for us to notice.

I'm incapable of finding meaning: Sometimes we convince ourselves that meaning is for other people—that we're the exception and we somehow missed the memo on how to live a meaningful life. But that's just fear talking. Meaning isn't a club you have to be invited to join. You engage with it. The more you pay attention to what matters to you, the more meaning starts showing up.

Practical Tips for Cultivating Everyday Meaning

Bringing a sense of meaning into your life doesn't have to be an epic quest. Sometimes, the deepest purpose is found in the smallest acts, the quiet moments, the spaces we already inhabit. Rather than a singular, grand vision, purpose is woven into the fabric of everyday life, found in the small moments and actions that give each day meaning. Here are some practical ways to uncover meaning right where you are.

Savor small moments: Meaning doesn't just show up in big achievements. It's in the little things. Notice the warmth of your morning coffee, the smile exchanged with a friend, or the satisfaction of finishing a task. Pay attention to what already fills your life with joy and depth. When you recognize meaning in these moments, you reinforce the idea that life is happening now—not at some distant point in the future when you've "figured it all out."

Reflect regularly: Set aside a few minutes each week to look back and consider what's bringing you meaning. Think about moments that made you feel connected, alive, or grateful. No need to analyze or critique your life—just notice what resonates. If something felt significant, ask yourself why. If something felt empty, consider what might be missing. Reflection helps us course-correct and ensure we're investing in the right things.

Align actions with values: Meaning grows when your daily actions reflect what truly matters to you. If you value connection, prioritize deep conversations over scrolling through social media. If you value creativity, carve out time to make something, even if it's just for you. If you value generosity, find small ways to give: your time, attention, or support. Identify one or two core values and ask yourself, "How am I living these today?" Small, intentional choices add up.

Embrace presence over pursuit: The search for meaning can become its own kind of distraction. The harder we chase it, the more it seems to slip away. Instead of treating meaning as something you need to find, focus on where it already exists. Breathe deeply. Be fully where you are. If you're having lunch with a friend, be in that

Your body isn't an obstacle. It's an ally—the strongest one you've ever had.

———————

conversation, not thinking about your to-do list. If you're reading a book, immerse yourself in the story, rather than feel guilty because you should be "doing something productive." The more present we are, the more we see that meaning has been here all along.

Nurture relationships: Few things bring deeper meaning than relationships. But relationships don't thrive on autopilot. They require attention, time, and care. Make space for meaningful conversations, check in on friends, and be intentional about who you surround yourself with. Research shows that strong relationships contribute to happiness and longevity, but beyond that, they provide the sense of belonging and connection that makes life feel significant. We don't create meaning alone.

Celebrate progress, not perfection: We often think meaning is tied to getting things right. But perfection is a moving target, and if we're constantly waiting to feel like we've arrived, we'll miss out on the meaning that comes from the process itself. If you're learning something new, celebrate the fact that you're stretching yourself. If you're navigating a challenging time, acknowledge that you're growing, even if it's a messy process. A meaningful life isn't one without struggle; it's one in which we recognize the value in the journey.

Let curiosity lead: Curiosity is one of the most underrated tools for discovering meaning. If something interests you, follow it. Try a new activity, ask deeper questions, explore ideas that intrigue you. Often, we feel stuck not because life lacks meaning but because we've stopped engaging with it. Staying curious keeps us connected, growing, and open to new sources of fulfillment.

Engage with contribution, not just consumption: One of the biggest shifts in midlife is realizing that meaning isn't just what we get; it's what we give. Mentoring someone younger in our field, volunteering our time, offering encouragement, sharing our experiences—these acts of generosity deepen our sense of purpose. Contribution doesn't require grand gestures or sweeping change. It happens in the small ways we make life better for others.

Recognize That Meaning Evolves

What felt meaningful at twenty-five might not feel the same at fifty. And that's okay. Meaning isn't fixed; it evolves as we do. Give yourself permission to reevaluate. If your career once provided a strong sense of purpose but now feels less fulfilling, explore what might come next. If your role in your family has shifted, look for new ways to connect. Rather than holding onto old definitions, midlife should be about recognizing when meaning is shifting and allowing something new to take shape.

The biggest mistake we make is waiting for meaning to arrive, as if one day we'll wake up with total clarity. But we build meaning moment by moment through the way we live, love, and engage with the world around us. It's already here, woven into the choices we make and the connections we nurture. The question isn't whether meaning exists in your life. It's whether you're noticing it.

TL;DR

- Meaning isn't something to chase; it's something to notice. It's already present in the relationships we nurture, the way we show up for others, and the small, everyday moments we often overlook.

- Midlife shifts our understanding of meaning. The achievements that once defined us may no longer feel as fulfilling. Meaning now comes from contribution, connection, and presence.

- Philosophy and science agree: A sense of purpose improves well-being, resilience, and even longevity. Meaning is essential for a satisfying life.

- Helpful mindsets can open the door to meaning. Seeing meaning in the everyday, creating it through our actions, and deepening relationships help us build a more fulfilling life.

- Common myths keep us stuck. We don't need a grand achievement or a perfectly defined purpose to lead meaningful lives. Meaning isn't in some distant future; it's in the choices we make today.

- Faith traditions and secular philosophies align more than we think. While different frameworks exist, the central truth remains: We're wired to seek purpose, to contribute, and to connect with something beyond ourselves.

- Practical steps matter. Savor small moments, reflect regularly, align actions with values, be present, nurture relationships, and recognize that meaning evolves over time.
- Meaning isn't waiting to be found. It's something we create, moment by moment, through the way we engage with the world.

PAUSE & REFLECT

- What moments in the past week have felt meaningful to you? What made them stand out?
- Are you searching for meaning in big achievements, or do you notice it in the everyday?
- What are your core values, and how do your daily actions reflect them?
- Are there relationships in your life that deepen your sense of meaning? How can you nurture them more?
- What small, intentional choices can you make today to cultivate more meaning in your life?

13

SHIFT INTO BEFRIENDING YOUR BODY
THE COMPANION THAT'S BROUGHT YOU HERE

Take care of your body. It's the only place you have to live.
JIM ROHN

Old Friend

This morning, like every morning,
my body woke up before I did,
already at work—
my heart keeping time,
my lungs rehearsing their symphony of air.
It doesn't complain—
about the late nights,
the skipped meals,

the way I treat it like
a slightly broken appliance
I'll get around to fixing someday.
My feet have carried me everywhere,
over uneven sidewalks,
through airports,
onto dance floors
where I embarrassed myself—
and them.
My stomach has been my faithful translator,
turning whatever I threw at it—
donuts, kale, tequila—
into fuel.
And yet, how often do I say thank you?
When have I sat down and said,
"I see you, I hear you,
I'm here for you too"?
Because this body,
my body,
is my closest ally,
my oldest friend.
And all it wants—
all it has ever wanted—
is for me to notice
that it's been here,
quietly,
carrying me through everything.

Shift into Befriending Your Body

FOR SO LONG, we've been told a story. That our bodies must be managed, shaped, shrunk, sculpted, optimized. That with enough discipline and willpower, we can mold them into whatever version of "good" we have been sold. But no matter how hard we try, the body refuses to be a before-and-after project. It keeps changing. It keeps speaking. It keeps asking us to listen. Instead of listening, we push harder. We override. We force it into submission.

Then midlife arrives. Suddenly, the rules we have lived by no longer seem to work. The body we have spent years trying to control has its own ideas. The metabolism slows, the joints stiffen, and the things we used to bounce back from take longer now.

A choice stands before us. Double down, keep forcing, try to out-discipline biology. Or shift. Treat the body as something to care for, nourish, strengthen, and enjoy.

This shift is no small thing. It means listening instead of silencing. Nourishing instead of neglecting. Moving because it feels good, not because we should. Your body is the quiet teammate that never stops showing up. Maybe it's time to return the favor. Midlife offers a chance to be in relationship with your body in a whole new way.

Ever had a friend who showed up when you least expected but most needed it? Maybe they knocked on your door with coffee after a long, impossible week. Maybe they sent a text—"Hey, you good?"—at exactly the right moment. And for a second, everything felt a little less heavy. A good friend shows up—consistently, not just when it's convenient. They listen, support, and remind you who you are, even when you forget. Now imagine if you treated your body the same way.

The Wake-Up Call

Maybe you're tempted to skip this chapter. Maybe you and your body are besties. Maybe you stretch every morning, drink your green smoothies, and listen to your body like it's an old friend. And if that's you, fantastic. Keep doing what you're doing. But that hasn't been my story.

This has been the hardest part of leading myself well. My biggest concern at midlife. It's where I've swung wildly between all-in and all-out. I've trained for half marathons, pushed myself hard, and then let it all slide. I've started and stopped a hundred times.

And then one day, I found myself in a dentist's chair, about to get a root canal. Routine procedure, no big deal. Until they took my blood pressure—and sent me home. Too high. So high. Then came the long journey to lower it.

That moment wasn't just about my health. It was about everything. The way I was pushing. The way I was ignoring. The way I was running on empty, assuming my body would just keep up. So I started paying attention and listening. And now, as I write this, I'm in a phase of real body care. I'm training for a Camino walk—something you can't just muscle your way through. It requires consistency, patience, and respect for what my body can do. I'm leading a team, which means I have to show up, train, and do the work. And it's changing me.

Because this time, I'm not managing my body; I'm partnering with it.

I used to see exercise as just another task on the list, something I had to do. But something is shifting. Now, I see it as both preparation and an act of care. It's not about looking a certain way or proving anything. It's about being ready. Ready to hike those hills. Ready to show up for my grandkids. Ready to feel good in my own skin.

From Lifespan to Healthspan

For years, we've measured success in birthdays. More candles on the cake, more years in the bank. But the real issue isn't how long we live—it's *how well* we live. That's the shift: from lifespan to healthspan. From just marking time to making time count. What good is a longer life if you spend it feeling sluggish, foggy, or disconnected? Focusing on your healthspan means showing up to your own life with strength, energy, and presence. It's moving through the years, not just being carried by them. And your body is on board. It rebuilds, renews, and rewires.

Aging is not a slow decline; it's a transition. Your body is in a constant state of *becoming*. Your skin renews every twenty-seven days. Your gut lining refreshes itself every few days. Your taste buds? Two weeks. Your bones completely remodel every decade. Your muscles rebuild. Your brain rewires. Your heart—both the one that beats and the one that *feels*—adapts, expands, and strengthens. You're designed for renewal.

This is where healthspan comes in. If your body is already wired for renewal, the real question is whether you are working with it or against it. Are you stacking small, life-giving habits that fuel your strength, clarity, and joy? Or are you just hoping to hold on, to avoid decline for as long as possible?

This is the shift. From waiting for breakdown to choosing to build up. From trying to not lose something to actively gaining more—more energy, more resilience, and more years when you feel alive. Healthspan isn't just staying in the game. It's playing fully—for as long as possible.

Your midlife body is adapting. To work with it rather than against it, you need to understand what's actually happening under the hood. Here's what you can expect as your body shifts in midlife, according to science. (Note: What follows is not a comprehensive list by any means.)

Midlife Body Changes and How to Support Your Body

Midlife shows up in your body in ways you don't expect. One day you're feeling strong and capable, and the next you're wondering why your back hurts after sitting for too long. Your body speaks, and in midlife, it's got a lot to say. But here's the good news: You can listen, respond, and care for it in ways that keep it moving, thriving, and strong.

Slowing Metabolism

Your body burns fewer calories as the years go by—a couple of percentage points per decade. Not a crisis, just a shift. The muscles that once carried you effortlessly need a little more attention now.

- Do strength training twice, maybe three times a week. Build muscle, and you'll keep the fire burning.
- Eat more protein—think 0.6 grams per pound of body weight. Not a crazy amount, just enough to fuel your muscles.
- Move every day, such as short walks, stretching, and mobility work. The goal is to keep everything moving.
- Stay hydrated. Dehydration can slow metabolism further.

Muscle Loss

Sarcopenia—muscle loss—sounds like a spell from a wizard's book. But it's not magic. It's what happens when muscle slowly fades if we don't use it.

- Lift things. Strength training helps retain and rebuild muscle.
- Prioritize protein, especially post-workout, to support muscle repair.
- Hydrate and rest—muscles need both to recover and grow.

When we pause,
we don't lose
momentum.
We gain direction.

———————

- Include balance and flexibility exercises to prevent injury and maintain mobility.

Hormonal Shifts
Estrogen declines in women and testosterone drops in men. The result? More fat, less muscle, mood swings, and energy dips.

- Strength training and protein intake help regulate hormones and maintain muscle.
- Prioritize sleep. Poor sleep disrupts hormones further.
- Manage stress—not by pushing it aside, but by addressing it. Meditation, deep breathing, and time outdoors all help.
- Consider adaptogens like ashwagandha and maca, which may support hormonal balance.
- If symptoms get in the way of daily life, seek medical support.

Drop in Bone Density
Bones lose about one percent of their density each year after fifty. If you're a postmenopausal woman, that rate is even higher.

- Weight-bearing exercises—walking, jogging, lifting, and moving—stimulate bone growth.
- Take calcium (1,200 mg daily) and vitamin D (600 to 800 IU daily) to support bone strength.

- Strength training helps by putting stress on bones, prompting them to rebuild stronger.
- Incorporate magnesium and vitamin K2, which help with calcium absorption.

Sleep Disruptions

Melatonin declines and hormones fluctuate. Sleep becomes this elusive thing you used to take for granted.

- Stick to a consistent bedtime and wake-up time. Routine is your friend.
- Limit screens before bed. Blue light suppresses melatonin.
- Cut caffeine after noon—yes, even if you think it doesn't affect you.
- Try magnesium, breathwork, and relaxation techniques to calm the nervous system.
- Reduce alcohol intake. It disrupts sleep cycles even if it helps you fall asleep initially.

Gut Changes

Your digestion isn't what it used to be. The gut microbiome shifts, and food might hit differently.

- Eat fiber-rich foods—vegetables, fruits, and whole grains—to keep digestion moving.
- Add fermented foods like yogurt, kimchi, and sauerkraut to support gut health.

- Stay hydrated. Water helps with digestion and nutrient absorption.
- Reduce processed foods and excess sugar, which can negatively impact gut bacteria.
- Experiment with probiotics and prebiotics for extra gut support.

Brain Aging

The processing speed slows, but wisdom and emotional intelligence? Those only grow.

- Move your body. Cardio boosts blood flow to the brain and sharpens memory.
- Learn new things—read, create, or take up a new hobby. Your brain loves novelty.
- Stay socially connected. Loneliness is a major risk factor for cognitive decline.
- Prioritize quality sleep, since your brain cleans itself and consolidates memory during deep sleep.
- Challenge your brain with puzzles, strategy games, or learning a new language.

This body of yours has been with you through every season, every milestone, and every change. Now it's asking for a little more care and attention. When you give it what it needs, it carries you forward, strong and steady, into everything still to come.

The Shift: From Old Stories to New Truths

We all carry stories about our relationship with our bodies. Some were handed to us. Some we picked up along the way. In midlife, those stories either hold us back or set us free. Maybe it's time for a rewrite.

Old Story: My best days are behind me.
New Truth: My body isn't breaking down; it's adapting. Strength, flexibility, and energy are still on the table.

Old Story: I don't have time to take care of myself.
New Truth: Taking care of my body isn't an extra—it's *foundational*. It's how I show up fully for everything and everyone that matters.

Old Story: I have to push through, no matter what.
New Truth: Rest isn't quitting. It's strategy. My body needs care, not punishment.

Old Story: I need to look perfect to be healthy.
New Truth: Health isn't a dress size. It's how I move, how I feel, and how I live.

Old Story: It's too late to change.
New Truth: My body was made for renewal. Muscles rebuild. Cells regenerate. Growth is always possible.

The stories we tell ourselves matter. The best part is we get to rewrite them.

The Shift: From Should to Want

There's something freeing about moving your body because you want to, not because you "should." When movement is a choice, not an obligation, it becomes a gift instead of a task. That shift changes everything. Imagine a relationship with your body built on trust rather than guilt. Where movement feels energizing, not punishing. Where eating well is fueling yourself, not fixing yourself. Where rest is something you honor, not something you have to earn.

It starts with small moments. A walk because the fresh air feels good. A deep stretch that wakes you up. Drinking water and actually noticing how much better you feel. Choosing foods that make you feel strong and clear-headed. Not having that glass of wine with dinner and waking up feeling sharper, more positive. These little choices add up—not in a way that demands perfection, but in a way that builds consistency, confidence, and care.

Here's the best part: When you start listening to your body, it responds. It strengthens, adapts, and carries you forward.

Befriending Your Body: A New Approach

Your body is an ally, not an obstacle. It's been with you every step of your life, adjusting, healing, and supporting you in ways you probably haven't even noticed. Now you have an opportunity to step into the next chapter with a new mindset of collaboration and respect, rather than one of control and criticism. The best relationships aren't built on demands. They're built on trust. The same is true for your relationship with your body. When you shift from pushing to listening, from forcing to supporting, you create something sustainable and freeing. Something better.

Exercise isn't just fitness; it's freedom. It's about waking up with energy, being able to lift, carry, climb, play, and move through life with ease. It's feeling good now, not chasing an ideal. The goal is to create a body that lets you do the things you love for as long as possible, whether that's hiking with friends, keeping up with your kids or grandkids, dancing at a wedding, or simply waking up feeling strong. You don't have to go big. Just start with what feels good. A short walk. A stretch in the sun. A moment to breathe deeply. The best movement is the kind that brings joy, because joy is what makes it last.

The Long Game: A Relationship That Lasts

Caring for your body is a lifelong partnership. And your body *wants* to work with you. It's designed for renewal, adaptation, and strength.

The goal isn't perfection. It's presence. It's making choices that support you today and build a foundation for tomorrow. It's knowing that every step—no matter how small—counts. And when you make that shift—when you move from seeing your body as something to fight to something to support—that's when everything changes. You stop chasing an end goal and start building a lifelong relationship. One built on care and trust, and one that keeps getting better.

TL;DR

- Your body is not a project to fix. It's a lifelong companion that thrives on care, not control.

- Aging is an adaptation. Your body is constantly renewing, rebuilding, and evolving.

- Movement is a gift. Find what feels good and energizes you, instead of forcing what you "should" do.

- Healthspan matters more than lifespan. It's living with strength, energy, and presence.

- Rest and nourishment are non-negotiable. Recovery is the foundation for longevity.

- Rewrite the old narratives. Let go of unrealistic expectations and embrace a mindset of trust and respect for your body.

- Small, consistent choices lead to lasting change. Every step—every stretch, every deep breath, and every moment of self-care—counts.

- Your body is already showing up for you. Now it's time to show up for it.

PAUSE & REFLECT

- What is one old story you've been telling yourself about your body? How can you rewrite it into something more supportive?

- When was the last time you truly listened to your body? What was it asking for?

- What movement feels good to you—not what you "should" do, but what you *want* to do?

- How can you start treating your body the way you'd treat a good friend?

14
SHIFT INTO STILLNESS
THE WORLD WON'T STOP, BUT YOU CAN

I have discovered that all the unhappiness of men arises from one single fact: that they cannot stay quietly in their own chamber.
BLAISE PASCAL

Finding the Quiet

There is a quiet waiting for you—
not in some distant place,
not at the end of a long-earned retreat,
but here, in the pause between one breath
and the next,
in the way the trees stand
without apology, without hurry,
rooted in the knowing that all things come and go.

> The stream does not rush to be anything
> other than itself.
> It carries what it must,
> drops what it does not need,
> and moves forward,
> not because it has to,
> but because it was made to move.
> And you—
> you have been moving for so long,
> chasing, holding, proving,
> as if the world would stop turning
> if you stopped for a moment to listen.
> But here is the truth:
> The world does not ask you to carry so much.
> It asks only that you arrive.
> That you sit.
> That you breathe.
> That you remember—
> everything you have been looking for
> is already here.

THE INVITATION TO STILLNESS doesn't arrive with fanfare. It slips in quietly, almost hidden beneath the ceaseless hum of a world that never stops. It's the whisper under the ping of emails, the endless scroll of social media, the clatter of obligations stretching from dawn to dark. The noise is constant, pulling us in every direction, tempting us to believe that busyness is where life's meaning resides.

But what if we stepped back? What if we paused, even for a moment?

Stillness isn't about escaping the noise entirely—that's impossible. It's about creating space within it, finding moments to breathe deeply and feel fully, to let clarity, creativity, and peace rise above the chaos. As Pico Iyer, author of *The Art of Stillness*, reminds us, "In an age of speed, I began to think, nothing could be more invigorating than going slow. In an age of distraction, nothing can feel more luxurious than paying attention."

Stillness is a choice to pause, step back, and be present. It requires intention, a willingness to sit with what is instead of reaching for what's next. John O'Donohue, the Irish poet and philosopher, wrote in *Anam Cara*, "Stillness is vital to the world of the soul. If as you age you become more still, you will discover that stillness can be a great companion." A companion. Not a void. Not something to fix or fill, but a space where life settles, where we reconnect with ourselves, and where clarity returns. Stillness is where we heal, where we listen, and where we come back to what truly matters.

There is so much discussion about mindfulness these days—meditation apps, breathing techniques, journaling prompts. But at its core, mindfulness is a return to being fully present. The Stoics knew this well. Marcus Aurelius wrote, "Nowhere you can go is more peaceful—more free of interruptions—than your own soul." Mindfulness isn't eliminating stress or achieving perfect calm; it's meeting each moment with presence and intention.

The Science of Stillness

Scientific research backs the benefits of mindfulness, showing it reduces stress, enhances emotional regulation, and improves cognitive function. We now know that deliberate moments of stillness—practices like meditation, focused breathing, or simply sitting in silence—have measurable effects on the body and the brain. When you slow down, you activate the parasympathetic nervous system, which regulates heart rate, lowers blood pressure, and reduces stress hormones like cortisol. These are essential biological responses that directly improve your health and well-being.

In terms of cognitive function, stillness enhances attention, working memory, and emotional regulation. Leading researchers have shown that even short daily practices can improve our ability to focus and reduce reactivity. The benefits extend to decision-making, conflict resolution, and long-term goal pursuit—all of which are key components of effective leadership, both personal and professional.

Stillness also plays a powerful role in how we relate to ourselves and others. It increases self-awareness and allows us to observe our thoughts and behaviors without immediate reaction. That space between stimulus and response? That's where emotional maturity lives. It's where growth happens.

Perhaps most compelling is the research showing that consistent stillness practices actually change traits. People become more compassionate, more resilient, and more capable of aligning their actions with their values.

This isn't just about feeling better. It's about becoming better.

In a world that rewards speed, stillness is a radical act. But it's not a retreat from responsibility—it's how we learn to carry it better. If you want to deepen your effectiveness and feel more connected, more present, and more aligned with what matters, begin by reclaiming stillness.

For readers who want to dive into the supporting studies, I've gathered resources and research links on the *Shift* website. But the core idea is simple: If you want to be stronger, start by being still.

Here are a few practical ways to cultivate mindfulness in daily life:

Mindful breathing: Pause and take three deep breaths, fully feeling the inhale and exhale. This simple act can reset your nervous system.

Body awareness: Scan your body for tension and intentionally release it. This practice can decrease physical stress and increase self-awareness.

Observation without judgment: Notice your thoughts as they arise, without clinging to or resisting them. This enhances emotional resilience.

Single-tasking: Focus on one activity at a time, whether eating, walking, or listening. This increases attention span and reduces mental fatigue.

Gratitude practice: Take a moment each day to acknowledge something you're grateful for. Research shows this practice increases overall well-being.

Helpful and Unhelpful Mindsets Around Stillness

The way we think about stillness determines how we experience it. Here are some helpful and unhelpful mindsets to consider.

Helpful Mindsets

Stillness is productive: Clarity and creativity emerge when we give ourselves space to pause.

I don't have to earn rest: Stillness is a human need, not a luxury reserved for after work is done.

Slowing down isn't falling behind: It allows for recalibration and better decision-making.

Presence is powerful: True engagement with the moment leads to richer experiences and relationships.

Silence is not empty; it's full of answers: When we stop filling every gap with noise, insights arise naturally.

Unhelpful Mindsets

Stillness is laziness: In reality, it enhances focus and efficiency rather than diminishing them.

I'll be still when I have time: If we wait for stillness to fit into our schedules, it never will.

Doing nothing is unproductive: Some of the best ideas and solutions surface when we stop forcing them.

I have to meditate perfectly for it to count: Even brief moments of quiet can be transformative.

If I'm still, I'll fall behind: The most effective leaders and thinkers know the value of intentional pauses.

The Gifts of Stillness

In these moments, something shifts. The clutter clears, and what matters comes into focus. Stillness is more than a pause; it's a return. Mary Oliver, another powerful voice on stillness, wrote, "Attention is the beginning of devotion." When we slow down, we don't lose momentum; we regain direction. When we embrace stillness, we uncover gifts we didn't know were there.

Clarity of thought: Stillness cuts through the mental fog, allowing deep thinking to thrive. Decisions stop being guesswork and start becoming confident, purposeful steps forward.

Self-awareness: In stillness, we begin to notice our motives, emotions, and patterns. We step outside the whirlwind and observe ourselves with curiosity rather than judgment.

Emotional resilience: It's in stillness that we learn to respond instead of react. Life's challenges lose their sting when we meet them with calm intention.

Creativity: In the quiet, our minds wander to places they rarely go. New ideas emerge, hidden connections reveal themselves, and solutions take shape effortlessly.

Deeper relationships: Stillness makes us more present for others. It shifts interactions from surface-level to deeply meaningful.

Purposeful action: It's not about stopping; it's about aligning our actions with our values. We move from busyness to meaningful work.

Inner peace: In stillness, we stop striving to prove ourselves. We find that we are enough—not because we've done everything, but because we've made space to simply be.

The Invitation to Wake Up

Stillness is a choice, a bold, deliberate act of saying, "This moment matters. I matter." When we make that choice, everything shifts. Clarity cuts through the fog. Creativity flows. Peace—real, deep peace—settles in. Right now, at this stage of life, that choice matters more than ever. We're waking up. Time feels different now—less chasing, more aligning. Less proving, more being.

Stillness isn't stepping away; it's stepping in. Tuning in to the wisdom we've gathered, the truths we've brushed past. Creating space to choose, intentionally, what comes next. This is where life hums. Where things click. Where we move forward, with meaning. Fully awake. Fully alive.

TL;DR

- Stillness allows us to recalibrate, refocus, and move forward with clarity.
- It's not about escaping the noise; it's about creating space within it. Even a brief pause can reset the mind.
- Stillness is an active choice. Rather than being passive, it enhances decision-making, creativity, and resilience.
- Mindful moments don't have to be perfect. A deep breath, a slow sip of coffee, or a quiet walk counts.
- Stillness shifts how we engage with life. It moves us from reacting to responding, from chasing to aligning.
- Presence is powerful. Showing up fully—rather than rushing through—creates richer experiences and deeper relationships.
- Slowing down isn't falling behind. It helps you move forward. Stillness creates the clarity and energy needed for what lies ahead.
- Stillness leads to clarity, creativity, and connection. When we pause, we don't lose momentum; we regain direction.

PAUSE & REFLECT

- Where in your day can you create even a small pocket of stillness?
- How can you practice mindfulness in a way that feels natural, not forced?
- What's one moment today where you can pause before reacting?
- How might embracing stillness help you reconnect with what truly matters?
- What's one simple way you can build stillness into your routine without overcomplicating it?

Optional Further Reading: Stillness, Mindfulness, and Reflection

If you're drawn to the idea of stillness and mindfulness and want to explore it more deeply, here are a few voices worth turning to.

John O'Donohue: His books *Anam Cara* and *To Bless the Space Between Us* explore the beauty of stillness, blessing, and reflection.

Mary Oliver: Her poetry, especially in *Devotions* and *A Thousand Mornings*, captures the wonder of quiet attention.

David Whyte: In *Consolations*, he reflects on presence and the necessity of pauses in life.

Pico Iyer: *The Art of Stillness* offers a modern perspective on why slowing down is essential.

Thich Nhat Hanh: *The Miracle of Mindfulness* and *Peace Is Every Step* are profound guides to embracing the present moment.

Richard Wagamese: *Embers: One Ojibway's Meditations* is a stunning collection of reflections on presence, wisdom, and healing.

Jon Kabat-Zinn: *Wherever You Go, There You Are* and *Full Catastrophe Living* offer foundational mindfulness practices for daily life.

Eckhart Tolle: *The Power of Now* is a foundational book on presence and mindfulness.

Thomas Merton: *New Seeds of Contemplation* explores deep, contemplative stillness from a Christian monastic perspective.

Richard Rohr: *Everything Belongs* blends spirituality with presence and wholeness.

15

SHIFT INTO BRAVE
CULTIVATE THE COURAGE TO SHIFT

If you are willing to feel everything, you can do anything.
PETER BREGMAN

Into the Murmur

It starts with a murmur,
a tummy rumble,
sweaty palms,
a stirring deep inside,
a sense that where you are
isn't where you're meant to stay.
Ahead, a path with no signs,
shadows thick and steady,
bushes that taunt and prick,
but there's a spark inside,

> an ember holding steady,
> even when doubt blows hard.
> To move beyond,
> to walk where comfort fades,
> trusting the ground beneath,
> knowing that beyond fear
> you'll stand tall,
> rooted in the strength
> of who you're becoming.

COURAGE IS that quiet, insistent voice that calls us toward something new—a step forward onto a path we've not taken before (or not recently, anyway). It's a force that nudges us out of the familiar, inviting us to break from routine and explore the unknown, even if it means leaving comfort behind. Courage isn't always about bold, heroic acts; sometimes it's making a subtle shift, opening a door we've always walked past, or simply being willing to reconsider a long-held belief. It's the willingness to entertain the idea of change, to imagine life beyond the current script.

People say they hate change, but I'm not sure that's true. What we really hate is uncertainty and being bad at something new. We hate the awkwardness, the fumbling, and the feeling of not knowing what we are doing. Change is not the enemy. It's the early stages of change that rattle us.

Change in midlife feels different. It's less like speeding across the surface in a powerboat and more like learning to sail. You can't rush it. You have to read the currents, work with the wind, and move in rhythm with forces bigger than you. At first, it feels slower, harder to steer. But in time, you realize the journey is richer, deeper, and far more beautiful than you imagined.

Not everyone hears the call to change in the same way. For some, change arrives as a necessity—a mountain that must be climbed. For others, like me, the harder task is not always leaping forward but in holding steady and staying rooted when every instinct wants to chase something new.

This chapter will meet you wherever you are on the path. Some readers may need the courage to move toward something unknown. Others may need the courage to stay and deepen their roots right where you are. Both require the same brave work: tuning in, trusting yourself, and listening closely to your inner voice that knows when it's time to stretch forward and when it's time to stay still and strong. Courage doesn't dissolve once you've made the decision to change or stay. That's when the real work begins. Whether you're transforming your life step by step or holding your ground with disciplined restraint, it takes sustained effort. The first step is only the start. The real journey begins when the excitement fades and you're left with the quiet persistence to keep walking.

The Comfort Trap

Comfort is incredibly appealing. It's that cozy duvet on a cold night, the familiar routine that requires no extra effort, the path of least resistance. It's easy to get lost in the allure of binge-watching, sinking into the couch as the next episode autoplays. There's something undeniably soothing about digging into a pint of Ben & Jerry's after a tough day—the creamy deliciousness that momentarily melts away stress. The comfort of a steady nine-to-five job; the security of a biweekly paycheck that comes like clockwork—even when, deep down, you know it's not fueling your passion.

We often find comfort in the mindless scroll of social media, checking out of reality for a bit, getting lost in other people's lives while the minutes slip away unnoticed. We stick with the same social circle we've had for years because it's easy, familiar, and doesn't require us to step out of our comfort zone. That gym membership? It's there, but the comfort of staying in bed or on the couch usually wins out over the discomfort of pushing ourselves physically. Even our daily routines, so predictable and safe, can become prisons of monotony, trapping us in cycles of mediocrity.

Then there's the big one—the dream deferred. You know the one: the book you've always wanted to write, the business idea you keep on the back burner, or the career change you daydream about. But pursuing that dream means stepping into the unknown and leaving behind the comfort of what you know. So you tell yourself, "I'll start next year," or, "When things settle down," all the while knowing that comfort is just fear in disguise, holding you back from what you're truly capable of.

These comforts, while they offer immediate gratification, come at a cost. They keep us from growth, from pushing our boundaries, and from stepping into the person we're meant to be. The shift from comfort to courage is about recognizing these traps, understanding that they offer only short-term relief, and choosing instead to step into the discomfort, the challenge, and the unknown. Because it's in those spaces that real growth, fulfillment, and success reside.

Courage isn't the absence of fear; it's feeling that fear and moving forward anyway. It's understanding that comfort can offer safety, but it can also keep you from growing. To grow, you have to be willing to step out into the unknown, to embrace the discomfort of change and trust that this journey will lead you toward the life you want. This is where your true power lies—in the courage to step beyond the familiar and into the life that's waiting for you.

The Courage to Trust Yourself

At the core of courage lies self-trust. Trusting yourself means listening to your inner wisdom, believing in your ability to navigate the unknown, and knowing that you can handle whatever comes next. It's easy to

Courage is feeling the fear **and choosing to move forward anyway.**

second-guess yourself, look outward for validation, and wait for a sign that you're making the right choice. But true courage comes from looking inward, acknowledging your fears, and moving forward anyway. Self-trust is built over time, through small acts of bravery. Each time you make a decision that aligns with your values, each time you take a risk in the direction of growth, you reinforce your ability to trust yourself. The more you practice, the stronger this trust becomes, until it forms the foundation upon which courage is built.

One of the greatest acts of courage is believing that you are enough, just as you are. That you don't need permission, validation, or a perfect plan to take the next step. That you are capable of handling the unknown, facing challenges, and growing through discomfort. Because when you trust yourself fully, you unlock a level of courage that no external reassurance can ever provide.

The Courage to Keep Going

Courage begins with persistence. It's staying the course when progress is slow, when doubt creeps in, and when setbacks make you question everything. True courage is showing up again and again, despite the uncertainty, fear, and difficulty. Every great change, every transformation, and every meaningful endeavor requires resilience. It requires the willingness to keep moving, even when the path is unclear. The courage to continue, even when the outcome is uncertain.

The Courage to Live Fully

Courage involves leaning into discomfort. A quote from my friend and author Peter Bregman transformed the way I see courage: "If you are willing to feel everything, you can do anything." I opened the chapter with this quote because it landed hard. And it hasn't let go because it speaks to something I keep learning over and over again. At first glance, it might sound like a motivational catchphrase, but it's actually a profound truth about human behavior. When you break it down, everything we do—every choice we make—is ultimately an attempt to either feel something or avoid feeling something.

Think about it. We stay in jobs we've outgrown not because we love them, but because we want to avoid the anxiety of uncertainty. We put off difficult conversations not because we don't have the words, but because we fear the discomfort of conflict or rejection. We scroll, binge-watch, overwork, overeat—not because these things truly satisfy us, but because they temporarily numb us from feeling something deeper. We are wired to seek pleasure and avoid pain. But when avoiding pain becomes the priority, we shrink our lives down to what feels safe. And safety, while comfortable, is rarely fulfilling.

This is why Peter's quote is transformational: It turns the equation upside down. Instead of making decisions based on what feels easiest in the moment, we choose to feel everything—to allow discomfort, fear, vulnerability, and even grief to exist. Because when we do, we unlock a new kind of freedom. Suddenly, we're not held hostage by our emotions. We don't need to stay stuck. We can move forward, not because we're fearless, but because we're willing to feel fear and keep going anyway.

What Research Says About Courage

Science, it turns out, has a lot to say about courage—more than we might think. At its core, courage isn't just a feeling or an abstract concept; it's a physiological process that involves our brain, nervous system, and our emotions. When we face a situation that scares us, the amygdala, the part of the brain responsible for processing fear, lights up. Courage helps us face that fear and move forward. The prefrontal cortex, the part of the brain that handles decision-making and reasoning, steps in to override the fear response, allowing us to act despite the fear. It's this dance between fear and reason that defines courage on a neurological level.

What's fascinating is that the more we engage in acts of courage, the more we can actually rewire our brains. Neuroplasticity—the brain's ability to change and adapt—means that with each courageous act, we're strengthening the neural pathways that help us face fear. It's like the brain's way of saying, "Hey, we've been here before. We can handle this." Over time, this repeated practice makes it easier to act courageously, even in situations that might have paralyzed us before. The fear doesn't disappear, but our ability to navigate it improves.

And there's more. Research shows that courage is contagious. When we witness someone else acting with courage, it activates similar neural circuits in our own brains, almost as if we're the ones taking that bold step. This is the science behind why stories of bravery inspire us: They literally light up the same pathways in our minds. These pathways remind us that we're all connected and that the courage of one can ripple out to others, creating a kind of collective bravery that's bigger than any one of us.

Courage Helps Us Bounce Back

Courage and resilience go hand in hand. Resilience is bouncing back from setbacks, and courage gives us the push to face our fears and stresses head-on. When life throws its hardest punches, courage keeps us standing, helping us navigate through the storm. Research shows that this combination of courage and resilience not only makes it easier to recover but also strengthens us for whatever comes next. This cycle of facing fears, bouncing back, and growing stronger propels us forward in life.

Courage Drives Change

Change is one of the hardest things we face, and it takes a lot of courage to start—and stick with—new habits or behaviors. The process of change is rarely smooth; it's full of uncertainty, difficulty, and the fear of the unknown. But courage is what keeps us moving through it. Whether it's quitting a bad habit, starting something new, or stepping into a role we've never tried before, courage helps us navigate the twists and turns of transformation. It's the force that drives change, allowing us to break free from what's familiar and embrace what's possible.

The Power of Support

Courage doesn't happen in a vacuum. Having a strong support system makes it easier to be courageous. When we know we have people backing us up, the risks of taking bold actions don't seem as big. Research highlights how important it is to have a community that encourages and supports us in being brave. It's in these relationships that we find the strength to take the leaps we might not take on our own.

Courage, then, isn't just about heroic moments; it's about the everyday choices we make, the people we surround ourselves with, and the ongoing dance between fear and action. Science tells us that courage is deeply woven into who we are, shaping how we grow, how we stand up for what matters, and how we drive the changes that lead to a fuller, more authentic life.

Mindsets That Drive Growth

Growth requires movement: If you're not moving, you're stuck. Progress isn't about getting everything right the first time; it's about continuously learning, adjusting, and acting.

You have more control than you think: Too many people wait for permission. You don't need it. You are already in control of what happens next. Every decision—big or small—has the power to shape your future.

Fear and growth are partners: Fear isn't something to eliminate; it's something to work with. If you're scared, it means you're standing on the edge of something important. Instead of letting fear stop you, use it as motivation to step forward.

Courage is a daily decision: It's not about being fearless, but about moving forward even with fear by your side. The people who create meaningful change are the ones who choose every day not to let fear control them.

Trust the process of change: Transformation doesn't happen overnight. Just because you don't see progress doesn't mean it's not happening. Keep showing up, keep doing the work, and trust that growth is unfolding beneath the surface.

Resilience is built through struggle: Every obstacle is part of your transformation. Growth comes when you face challenges head-on, learning to move through them instead of around them. Each setback is like a layer that builds you up and makes you stronger for whatever lies ahead.

Believe in your own potential: Self-doubt is the biggest roadblock to change. If you don't believe in your ability to grow, you'll hesitate at every turn. But here's the truth: You are capable of far more than you think. Trust yourself, and act accordingly.

Comparison is a losing game: Your path is yours alone. The fastest way to lose momentum is to measure your progress against someone else's. Focus on what's in front of you and keep moving forward.

Courage is contagious. When we witness an act of courage, the same pathways light up in our brains.

Mindsets That Keep You Stuck

Comfort is safety: Staying where things feel easy and familiar might seem like the smart choice, but real growth only happens when you're willing to push beyond what's comfortable.

It's too risky: Everything carries some level of risk—including staying exactly where you are. The question isn't whether change is risky. It's whether the risk of doing nothing is even greater.

I don't have control: Feeling powerless is a mindset, not a reality. You have more control than you think. Every decision—big or small—is a chance to shift your trajectory.

I'm waiting for the right time: The perfect moment doesn't exist. If you wait for conditions to be just right, you'll stay in the same place forever. Start now, with what you have, and figure it out as you go.

Discomfort is a red light: Discomfort doesn't mean stop. It's proof that you're stepping into something new. Don't let it hold you back.

Practical Tips for Change

Start with why—then hold onto it: Without a strong why, change feels like chaos. Your why is your anchor—it keeps you steady when things get hard. Write it down. Keep it close. Let it drive you forward. When you know your purpose, it's easier to stay committed even when things get tough.

Small steps, big impact: The first step doesn't need to be big. It just needs to happen. One step today, another tomorrow. That's how momentum builds, and momentum is what makes change stick.

Recognize your choice points: Every day, you make decisions that shape your future. Some are obvious, while others are subtle. The key is learning to recognize those moments of choice—the ones where you can step forward into the unknown or retreat to what's familiar. Progress happens when you lean into those moments with intention.

Surround yourself with people who challenge and support you: The people in your life either push you forward or keep you stuck. Seek out those who challenge you to grow, support you when things get tough, and remind you of what's possible. Change isn't easy, but with good people by your side, it becomes a whole lot more achievable.

Discomfort is proof you're growing: If you're waiting for change to feel comfortable, you'll be waiting forever. Discomfort is a signal that you're stretching beyond your limits. Instead of avoiding it, embrace it. It means you're stepping into something bigger.

Pause, reflect, and adjust: Change isn't a straight line. There will be moments when you need to stop, evaluate, and pivot. What's working? What's not? The best leaders and decision-makers aren't rigid; they adjust course when needed, without losing sight of the goal.

Lead yourself with kindness: You will stumble. You will doubt yourself. That's part of the process. But self-criticism won't get you anywhere. Treat yourself with the same patience and encouragement you would offer to a close friend.

Clarity comes in the quiet: Big decisions aren't made in a rush. Step away from the noise, take a breath, and let clarity emerge. Courage doesn't always require action; sometimes reflection is where it starts. When you make space for stillness, you gain perspective, and with perspective comes better choices.

Step Boldly Into What's Next

Transitions are a little like standing at the shoreline: You can't tell if the tide's coming in or going out. All you know is you're meant to be there, barefoot, feeling it. That pull toward possibility, the sense that there's more—not more to prove, not more to accumulate, but more *life* waiting for you to step into it.

You've spent years gathering wisdom, collecting experiences, and learning what matters and what doesn't. Now is the time to use it. To take everything you've been given, everything you've earned, and everything you've become—and move forward with intention. This is not an ending. It's not a winding down. This is an opening. A widening of perspective, a deeper engagement with what matters most. And the best part? You get to decide what you build, what you keep, and what you leave behind.

But here's the real invitation: to step forward not just with action, but with feeling. Courage isn't charging ahead without fear. It's allowing yourself to feel everything along the way and still keep moving forward. The uncertainty, the excitement, the grief, and the hope. The full, messy, beautiful range of emotions that come with change. Because when you let yourself feel it all, you unlock the kind of freedom that makes anything possible.

So take the step. Lean into the questions, the unknowns, and the dreams that won't let go of you. There is more ahead—more connection, more meaning, more depth, and more joy. The only thing standing between you and that life is a little courage. You're ready. You always have been. Now go.

TL;DR

- Courage is a choice. It's not being fearless; it's stepping forward despite the fear.
- Comfort can be a trap. What feels safe today might be holding you back from what's possible tomorrow.
- Trust yourself. The more you listen to your own wisdom and take action, the stronger your confidence grows.
- Growth happens in discomfort. If it feels uncertain, stretching, or even scary, you're probably on the right path.
- Small steps lead to big changes. Momentum builds when you take consistent, intentional action.
- Feel everything, then move forward. Avoiding discomfort keeps you stuck; facing it opens the door to real transformation.
- Persistence is courage in motion. Starting is one thing, but real courage is about showing up again and again.
- The best is still ahead. Your past has shaped you, but it doesn't define you. What comes next is up to you.

PAUSE & REFLECT

- Where in your life is comfort keeping you from growth?
- What small, courageous step can you take today?
- When was the last time you trusted yourself fully?
- What emotions are you avoiding that might actually be guiding you?
- If you knew you were ready, what would you do next?

CONCLUSION
THIS IS JUST THE BEGINNING

HERE WE ARE. At the end. And also at the edge.

Because that's how it works, right? Every ending is a beginning. Every door closing means something else is opening. You've made your way through these pages, letting them nudge you, pull at you, and maybe even shake you up a little. You've sat with these shifts, these invitations to see things differently, to loosen your grip, to step forward with new eyes.

Now, you stand at the threshold. This is where it gets real. This is where you decide if these words will stay right here, on the page, as ideas you once read, or if they'll become something more. Something living. Something that changes the way you wake up in the morning, the way you move through your day, the way you carry your past, and the way you step into your future.

Shifts only matter if they sink in, take root, and shape not just what you think but how you live.

You've encountered three powerful commitments: to lead yourself well, to tell yourself the truth no matter how uncomfortable it might be, and to embrace your story with radical acceptance. But let's be honest—just reading about these commitments doesn't mean you've made them. Change happens in action. In choice. So, will you?

Will you take these commitments and make them yours? Will you lead yourself with clarity and intention? Will you take an honest look at your life, your patterns, and your choices and tell yourself the truth? Will you embrace your story—all of it, the beautiful, the messy, the parts you wish were different, and the parts you're still figuring out?

These aren't abstract ideas. They're foundations. Anchors. Pillars that will hold you up as you navigate midlife and everything beyond. But only if you choose them.

And what about the seven mindset shifts? Curiosity. Connection. Response-Ability. Alignment. Body. Stillness. Bravery. Each one is a doorway, as well as a new way to see and a new way to live. But shifts are just words on a page until you choose them, plant them in the soil of your actual, everyday life, and give them the light and water they need to grow.

This isn't just poetry or inspiration. This is science. This is what we know about well-being, meaning, and what makes a life rich and deep and full. When you shift into curiosity, you open yourself up. You step into the unknown with wonder instead of fear. You trade certainty for discovery. And the research is clear: Curiosity leads to more happiness, engagement, connection, and a sense of being fully alive. When you shift into connection, you move beyond yourself. You reach for people, community, and the messy, beautiful reality that we're all in this together. Science backs this up too. Strong connections lead to longer lives, deeper joy, and greater resilience.

When you shift into the pause, you reclaim your power. You create space between what happens and how you respond. You decide who you want to be in the moment. People who practice this—who learn to pause—navigate stress better, suffer less, and live with more ease. And when you shift into alignment, you also connect to something deeper. You let your life reflect what truly matters. For some, that means a relationship with God. For others, it means stepping into mystery, into the vastness of existence, and into the questions that crack you open and pull you toward something bigger than yourself.

When you shift into your body, you honor it. You listen, move, and fuel it well. And the data is clear: How you treat your body affects everything—your energy, mood, clarity, and ability to engage with life fully. How you treat your mind also affects everything. When you shift into stillness, you create space. You listen for the quiet voice inside you, remember what matters, and let go of the noise. Studies show that people who practice stillness, meditate, and reflect experience less anxiety, more clarity, and a deeper sense of peace.

And when you shift into brave, you stop waiting for certainty. You step forward anyway. You say yes to change, to risk, and to the unknown. Here's what we know:

People who embrace courage and lean into change don't just survive life's transitions. They grow. They evolve. They thrive.

So, as you step forward from here, remember this: The path won't always be clear. The next step won't always be easy. But it's yours. And the life waiting for you? It's rich. It's full. It's bursting with possibility.

But only if you say yes.

ACKNOWLEDGMENTS

WRITING A BOOK is like embarking on a road trip with a destination in mind, only to discover that the journey takes you to places you never imagined. Along the way, you meet some extraordinary people who make the ride unforgettable. Let me take a moment to recognize those who've traveled this road with me.

First, to Jodi—my partner, my co-pilot in all of life's adventures. Thank you for your endless patience and steadfast support and for always knowing when it is time to pull over and take a break. You've been there through every twist and turn, reminding me to laugh, breathe, and take it all in. I couldn't have made it here without you.

To my kids, who fill my life with light and wonder—this book is for you as much as anyone else. And to my mom, my first teacher and constant cheerleader—your love and wisdom have shaped me in ways I can't begin to express. Thank you for always believing in me, no matter what.

To my team, huzzah! We did it. You stuck with me even when the road got rough. Your dedication, hard work, and ability to keep everything moving forward, even when the path wasn't clear, have been nothing short of amazing. We're on a mission to redefine what midlife can be, and I'm beyond grateful to have you alongside me.

To my friends, who checked in, asked the tough questions, and kept me focused—you've been the sounding boards and the reminders of why I started this journey. Thank you for your encouragement and curiosity and for keeping me grounded when I needed it most.

A special shout-out to a few wordsmiths who have been a part of this process. Mona Stuart, your insights are a gift. Annie Brandner, the sharp and thoughtful editor at *InHabit Magazine*, your thoughts have elevated this work. Alison Caldwell Johnston, thank you for helping crack the name code—your creativity and intuition are unparalleled.

A huge thank you to the team at Page Two, and especially to my editors, Scott Steedman and Jenny Govier. Your guidance was like a map when the road ahead was foggy. You helped shape this book into something I'm truly proud of, and I'm so grateful for your wisdom and support in bringing it to life.

And finally, to you—the reader. Thank you for picking up this book and taking a chance on me and this journey. Writing can feel like an isolated endeavor, but knowing you're out there makes it all worth it. We're in this together, navigating the ups and downs of midlife, and I'm honored that you've chosen to walk this path with me.

So here's to the journey, to the incredible people who make it worthwhile, and to the road that still lies ahead. Thank you, from the depths of my heart.

NOTES

Introduction: Setting the Stage

p. 11   *Writer Rich Cohen put it this way*: Rich Cohen, "The Ballad of Downward Mobility," *The Atlantic*, August 28, 2022, https://www.theatlantic.com/ideas/archive/2022/08/downward-economic-mobility-boomer-generation-x-debt/671260/.

p. 11   *Elwood Watson said it well*: Elwood Watson, "Generation X and the Spirit of Resiliency," Medium, June 19, 2021, https://medium.com/modernidentities/generation-x-and-the-spirit-of-resiliency-94b343c446fb.

p. 12   *Social scientist Arthur Brooks captures this perfectly*: Arthur C. Brooks, "The Two Choices That Keep a Midlife Crisis at Bay," *The Atlantic*, May 19, 2022, https://www.theatlantic.com/family/archive/2022/05/midlife-crisis-choices-opportunities/638427/.

p. 18   *Viktor Frankl... drew on Nietzsche's insight*: Friedrich Nietzsche, *Twilight of the Idols*, trans. Duncan Large (Oxford Paperbacks, 2008). Originally published in German in 1889 by C. G. Naumann.

p. 19   *As Jim Rohn said*: Jim Rohn (@OfficialJimRohn), "'Take care of your body. It's the only place you have to live.' —Jim Rohn," Facebook, September 11, 2016, https://www.facebook.com/OfficialJimRohn/posts/10157428873280635.

1. Life in Two Halves

p. 32   *Carl Jung captured this transition perfectly*: C. G. Jung, Modern Man in Search of Soul (Harcourt, Brace & World, 1933).

p. 33   *James Hollis... nails it when he says*: James Hollis, *Finding Meaning in the Second Half of Life: How to Finally, Really Grow Up* (Gotham Books, 2006).

p. 36   *Carl Jung is often quoted as saying*: See C. G. Jung, *Two Essays on Analytical Psychology*, trans. and ed. R. F. C. Hull and Gerhard Adler, vol. 7 of *The Collected Works of C. G. Jung* (Princeton University Press, 1972).

2. Mindset and Midlife

p. 43   *Carol Dweck's work shows us a simple truth*: Carol S. Dweck, *Mindset: The New Psychology of Success* (Random House, 2006).

4. Looking Inward to Look Outward

p. 69   *Dalai Lama offers a simple but powerful truth*: Dalai Lama, Desmond Tutu, and Douglas Abrams, *The Book of Joy: Lasting Happiness in a Changing World* (Avery, 2016).

p. 69   *Arthur Brooks calls it the second curve of happiness*: Arthur C. Brooks, *From Strength to Strength: Finding Success, Happiness, and Deep Purpose in the Second Half of Life* (Portfolio, 2022).

5. Navigating Midlife's Derailers

p. 77   *the small, everyday decisions that either align*: Joseph Ciarrochi, Ann Bailey, and Russ Harris, *The Weight Escape: How to Stop Dieting and Start Living* (Shambhala, 2014).

6. Commitment One

Epigraph: Jana Kingsford, *Unjuggled: Balance Is Not Something You Find, It's Something You Create* (published by the author, October 5, 2016), Kindle.

p. 88   *My friend Lisa Strogal calls this Whole Person intelligence*: "Our Team: Lisa Strogal," ShadowLight Global, accessed May 24, 2025, https://shadowlightglobal.com/wps-members/lisa-strogal/.

p. 88   *"I've participated in every bad decision I've ever made."*: "Leading Yourself Well," posted November 7, 2020, by Your Move with Andy Stanley, YouTube, 27 min., 58 sec., https://yourmove.is/videos/leading-yourself-well.

7. Commitment Two

Epigraph: "Thomas Jefferson to Nathaniel Macon, 12 January 1989," *Founders Online*, National Archives, Washington, DC, https://founders.archives.gov/documents/Jefferson/03-13-02-0511.

8. Commitment Three

Epigraph: David Marchese, "Michael J. Fox on Parkinson's, Taking the Wrong Roles and Staying Positive.," *The New York Times Magazine*, March 1, 2019, https://www.nytimes.com/interactive/2019/03/01/magazine/michael-j-fox-parkinsons-acting.html.

p. 117   *"owning every square inch of your story"*: Rob Bell, *We'll Get Back to You: A Play* (Backhouse Books, 2022).

p. 122   *the insights and experiences of Dr. Marsha Linehan*: Marsha M. Linehan, *Cognitive-Behavioral Treatment of Borderline Personality Disorder* (Guilford Publications, 1993).

9. Shift into Curiosity

Epigraph: Bob Goff (@bobgoff), "Embrace uncertainty. Some of the most beautiful chapters in our lives won't have a title until much later.," Twitter (now X), February 6, 2021, https://twitter.com/bobgoff/status/1358175944012300288.

p. 134   *Like Hamlet said to Horatio*: William Shakespeare, *Hamlet* (Penguin Classics, 2016).

p. 137   *"We do not think ourselves into new ways of living"*: Richard Rohr, *Falling Upward: A Spirituality for the Two Halves of Life* (Jossey-Bass, 2011).

p. 139   *Erik Erikson described midlife*: Erik H. Erikson, *Identity and the Life Cycle* (W. W. Norton, 1959).

10. Shift into Connection

Epigraph: Rick Warren, *The Purpose Driven Life: What on Earth Am I Here For?* (Zondervan, 2002), 148.

p. 147   *The Dalai Lama puts it plainly*: Dalai Lama, Tutu, and Abrams, *The Book of Joy*.

p. 148   *Harvard's eighty-five-year-long Study of Adult Development*: Robert Waldinger and Marc Schulz, *The Good Life: Lessons from the World's Longest Scientific Study of Happiness* (Simon & Schuster, 2023).

p. 148   *Research from the American Psychological Association shows that*: Kirsten Weir, "LifeSaving Relationships," *Monitor on Psychology* 49, no. 3 (March 2018): 46, https://www.apa.org/monitor/2018/03/life-saving-relationships.

p. 148   *Psychologist Shelley Taylor coined the phrase*: Shelley E. Taylor, *The Tending Instinct: How Nurturing is Essential to Who We Are and How We Live* (Henry Holt & Co., 2002).

p. 149   *"The value of our lives"*: Simon Sinek (@simonsinek), "The value of our lives is not determined by what we do for ourselves. The value of our lives is determined by what we do for others," Twitter (now X), October 20, 2020, https://x.com/simonsinek/status/1318599130076381191.

11. Shift into Response-Ability

Epigraph: Jonatan Mårtensson, "Feelings are much like waves, we can't stop them from coming but we can choose which one to surf," quoted on Goodreads, retrieved June 16, 2025, https://www.goodreads.com/quotes/670136-feelings-are-much-like-waves.

p. 163 *Daniel Goleman, the pioneer of emotional intelligence, has spent years*: Daniel Goleman, *Emotional Intelligence: Why It Can Matter More Than IQ* (Bantam Books, 1995).

p. 163 *Brené Brown shows us that*: Brené Brown, *Daring Greatly: How the Courage to Be Vulnerable Transforms the Way We Live, Love, Parent, and Lead* (Gotham Books, 2012).

p. 163 *Viktor Frankl, a Holocaust survivor and psychiatrist*: Viktor E. Frankl, *Man's Search for Meaning* (Beacon Press, 1962).

p. 167 *emotions aren't just automatic reactions*: Lisa Feldman Barrett, *How Emotions Are Made: The Secret Life of the Brain* (Houghton Mifflin Harcourt, 2017).

p. 168 *Gross studies cognitive reappraisal*: James J. Gross, "Emotion Regulation: Affective, Cognitive, and Social Consequences," *Psychophysiology* 39, no. 3 (May 2002): 281-91, https://doi.org/10.1017/s0048577201393198.

p. 168 *Porges's Polyvagal Theory*: Stephen W. Porges, *The Polyvagal Theory: Neurophysiological Foundations of Emotions, Attachment, Communication, and Self-Regulation* (W. W. Norton, 2011).

p. 168 *Kabat-Zinn teaches that mindfulness*: Jon Kabat-Zinn, *Full Catastrophe Living: Using the Wisdom of Your Body and Mind to Face Stress, Pain, and Illness* (Delta, 1990).

p. 168 *Davidson is known for research on neuroplasticity*: Richard J. Davidson and Sharon Begley, *The Emotional Life of Your Brain: How Its Unique Patterns Affect the Way You Think, Feel, and Live—and How You Can Change Them* (Hudson Street Press, 2012).

p. 179 *the core idea behind Internal Family Systems*: Richard C. Schwartz, *Internal Family Systems Therapy* (The Guilford Press, 1995).

12. Shift into Alignment

Epigraph: Frank Martela and Michael F. Steger, "The Three Meanings of Meaning in Life: Distinguishing Coherence, Purpose, and Significance," *The Journal of Positive Psychology* 11, no. 5 (2016): 531–45, https://doi.org/10.1080/17439760.2015.1137623.

p. 189 *Søren Kierkegaard believed that meaning isn't something we find*: Søren Kierkegaard, *The Sickness unto Death: A Christian Psychological Exposition for Upbuilding and Awakening*, trans. and ed. Edna H. Hong and Howard V. Hong (Princeton University Press, 1983).

p. 189 *Jean-Paul Sartre took this a step further*: Jean-Paul Sartre, *Existentialism Is a Humanism*, trans. Carol Macomber (Yale University Press, 2007).

p. 189 *Albert Camus introduced the idea of the absurd*: Albert Camus, *The Myth of Sisyphus* (Vintage International, 2018).

p. 192 *Dr. Michael Steger, a professor at Colorado State University*: "It Matters: The Science and Practice of a Meaningful Life," MentorCoach LLC, accessed June 17, 2025, https://www.mentorcoach.com/class/matters-science-practice-meaningful-life.

p. 192 *Psychological research has consistently found that*: Michael F. Steger, Patricia Frazier, Shigehiro Oishi, and Matthew Kaler, "The Meaning in Life Questionnaire: Assessing the Presence of and Search for Meaning in Life," *Journal of Counseling Psychology* 53, no. 1 (January 2006): 80–93, https://doi.org/10.1037/0022-0167.53.1.80; Nathan Mascaro and David H. Rosen, "Existential Meaning's Role in the Enhancement of Hope and Prevention of Depressive Symptoms," *Journal of Personality* 73, no. 4 (August 2005): 985–1014, https://doi.org/10.1111/j.1467-6494.2005.00336.x; Stephanie A. Hooker, Kevin S. Masters, and Crystal L. Park, "A Meaningful Life Is a Healthy Life: A Conceptual Model Linking Meaning and Meaning

Salience to Health," *Review of General Psychology* 22, no. 1 (March 2018): 11–24, https://doi.org/10.1037/gpr0000105.

p. 193 *Psychologists Carol Ryff and Burton Singer have reinforced these findings*: Carol D. Ryff and Burton Singer, "Flourishing Under Fire: Resilience as a Prototype of Challenged Thriving," in ed. Corey L. M. Keyes and Jonathan Haidt, *Flourishing: Positive Psychology and the Life Well-Lived* (American Psychological Association, 2003), 15–36.

p. 193 *a strong sense of purpose can even be a predictor of longevity*: Emily Esfahani Smith, *The Power of Meaning: Crafting a Life That Matters* (Crown, 2017).

p. 194 *Studies in positive psychology show that*: Crystal L. Park, "Making Sense of the Meaning Literature: An Integrative Review of Meaning Making and Its Effects on Adjustment to Stressful Life Events," *Psychological Bulletin* 136, no. 2 (March 2010): 257–301, https://doi.org/10.1037/a0018301; Patrick L. Hill and Sara J. Weston, "Evaluating Eight-Year Trajectories for Sense of Purpose in the Health and Retirement Study," *Aging & Mental Health* 23, no. 2 (2019): 233–37, https://doi.org/10.1080/13607863.2017.1399344; Paul T. P. Wong, "Meaning-Centered Counselling in Retirement," in ed. Paul T. P. Wong and Prem S. Fry, *The Human Quest for Meaning: A Handbook of Psychological Research and Clinical Applications* (Lawrence Erlbaum Associates, 1998), 395–435.

13. Shift into Befriending Your Body
Epigraph: Jim Rohn (@OfficialJimRohn), "'Take care of your body."

14. Shift into Stillness
Epigraph: Blaise Pascal, *Pensées*, trans. A. J. Krailsheimer (Penguin Classics, 1995). Originally published in French in 1670 by Guillaume Desprez.

p. 225   *"In an age of speed, I began to think"*: Pico Iyer, *The Art of Stillness: Adventures in Going Nowhere* (Simon & Schuster/TED, 2014).

p. 225   *"Stillness is vital to the world of the soul"*: John O'Donohue, *Anam Cara: A Book of Celtic Wisdom* (Harper Perennial, 1998).

p. 225   *"Nowhere you can go is more peaceful"*: Marcus Aurelius, *Meditations*, trans. Gregory Hays (Modern Library, 2003).

p. 229   *"Attention is the beginning of devotion"*: Mary Oliver, *Long Life: Essays and Other Writings* (Da Capo Press, 2004).

15. Shift into Brave

Epigraph: Peter Bregman, *Leading with Emotional Courage: How to Have Hard Conversations, Create Accountability, and Inspire Action on Your Most Important Work* (Wiley, 2018), XXVI.

p. 242   *"If you are willing to feel everything, you can do anything"*: Bregman, *Leading with Emotional Courage*.

BEYOND THE PAGES
BRINGING *SHIFT* TO LIFE

Shift is more than a book. It's a call to rethink, reimagine, and redefine your midlife experience. Here's how to join the journey and bring these ideas to life.

Step In

Explore InHabit.Life: Our coaching, counseling, retreats, courses, and discussion circles are designed for those ready to find deeper meaning and clarity in their middle years. Start your journey at www.inhabit.life.

Subscribe to *InHabit Magazine*

This is more than a magazine: It's a community—an online space for stories, insights, and real conversations on well-being, relationships, and finding fulfillment. Subscribe at www.inhabitmagazine.com and stay connected to a world of ideas.

Go Deeper

Join our online coaching circles on *Shift*: Imagine a book club, but better. Our *Shift* coaching circles are held online, combining the fun of reading with the depth of guided discussion. Led by skilled coaches, each circle explores key concepts from the book, shares personal insights, and supports your journey in real time.

Get personalized support: Work one-on-one with our experienced coaches and counselors who guide you with honesty and wisdom.

Join a retreat or online course: Take time to reflect and recharge. These are experiences crafted to inspire transformation through connection and shared insight.

Visit the *Shift* website: I worked hard to keep *Shift* uncluttered and focused, but I know some readers crave research and data. If you want to dive deeper into the studies and insights behind the book, this site is designed to scratch that itch. Explore additional resources, research, and tools to support your shift at www.shiftintomidlife.com.

Make *Shift* a Shared Journey

Share the book: Spread the message by sharing *Shift* with friends, family, and colleagues. Real change happens when we come together to learn, question, and grow. Consider gifting the book to someone who could benefit from reading it.

Leave a review: If *Shift* has resonated with you, consider leaving a review. Your thoughts help others discover the book and join this movement toward a more purposeful midlife.

Invite Me to Your Event

Let's connect on the big ideas: Interested in a keynote or fireside chat about meaning, resilience, and embracing change? I'd be honored to join you and your team. To book a speaking engagement, visit www.peterreek.com.

Thank you for stepping into this journey with me. Together, we're redefining midlife.

ABOUT THE AUTHOR

PETER REEK is not just an author, coach, educator, and business owner—he's a trailblazer in the wild and wonderful journey of midlife. With over three decades of diving deep into business leadership, recruitment, and coaching, Peter has rubbed shoulders with some of the most iconic brands on the planet—lululemon, Expedia, Mercedes, Nintendo. But it's not the logos that define him; it's the path he chose, one that led him away from the corporate grind and into the heart of what really matters: human experience.

After years of building businesses and leading teams across the globe, Peter heard a call—a deep, resonant one—to explore the bigger questions. The kind of questions that creep up in the quiet moments, when the hustle dies down and you start wondering about the things that

PHOTO: PETER HOLST PHOTOGRAPHY

really last. This led him to pursue a master's in applied positive psychology and coaching from the University of East London, where he threw himself into understanding what it means to truly live—fully, authentically—as we age.

From this deep well of passion, InHabit.Life was born. It's more than a project; it's a movement. A rallying cry to embrace midlife with all the adventure and possibility it holds. Through his writing, his coaching, and the community he's built, Peter invites us to see midlife not as a closing chapter, but as the beginning of something new, something powerful.

As an author, Peter's work is a bold declaration that the second half of life can be the most extraordinary part of the journey—a time for renewal, for growth, and for diving deep into the things that truly satisfy the soul.

www.ingramcontent.com/pod-product-compliance
Lightning Source LLC
Chambersburg PA
CBHW030230100526
44583CB00013BA/671